Cholesterol Measurement: Test Accuracy and Factors That Influence Cholesterol Levels

United States Government Accountability Office Program Evaluation and Methodology Division

The BiblioGov Project is an effort to expand awareness of the public documents and records of the U.S. Government via print publications. In broadening the public understanding of government and its work, an enlightened democracy can grow and prosper. Ranging from historic Congressional Bills to the most recent Budget of the United States Government, the BiblioGov Project spans a wealth of government information. These works are now made available through an environmentally friendly, print-on-demand basis, using only what is necessary to meet the required demands of an interested public. We invite you to learn of the records of the U.S. Government, heightening the knowledge and debate that can lead from such publications.

Included are the following Collections:

Budget of The United States Government
Presidential Documents
United States Code
Education Reports from ERIC
GAO Reports
History of Bills
House Rules and Manual
Public and Private Laws

Code of Federal Regulations
Congressional Documents
Economic Indicators
Federal Register
Government Manuals
House Journal
Privacy act Issuances
Statutes at Large

United States General Accounting Office

GAO

Report to the Chairman, Subcommittee on Investigations and Oversight, Committee on Science, Space, and Technology, House of Representatives

December 1994

CHOLESTEROL MEASUREMENT

Test Accuracy and Factors That Influence Cholesterol Levels

GAO/PEMD-95-8

United States
General Accounting Office
Washington, D.C. 20548

Program Evaluation and
Methodology Division

B-257298

December 30, 1994

The Honorable James A. Hayes
Chairman, Subcommittee on Investigations
 and Oversight
Committee on Science, Space, and
 Technology
House of Representatives

Dear Mr. Chairman:

In response to your request, we are submitting this report, which examines how cholesterol and its subfractions are measured in different laboratory settings and discusses what is known about the accuracy of these measurement techniques. The report also discusses various analytical and biological factors that can affect an individual's cholesterol levels. Furthermore, the report assesses the potential effect of cholesterol measurement variability and the classification and treatment of patients.

We are sending copies to interested congressional committees and government agencies, and we will make copies available to others upon request. If you have any questions or would like additional information, please call me at (202) 512-2900 or Kwai-Cheung Chan, Director of Program Evaluation in Physical Systems Areas, at (202) 512-3092. Major contributors to this report are listed in appendix II.

Sincerely yours,

Terry E. Hedrick
Assistant Comptroller General

Executive Summary

Coronary heart disease is a leading cause of death for Americans, and preventive measures have emphasized reducing risk factors such as high blood cholesterol levels. In 1985, the National Institutes of Health launched the National Cholesterol Education Program (NCEP) to encourage Americans to have their cholesterol measured and modify their diet and to provide clinical guidelines for identifying and treating persons who are particularly at high risk of heart disease. If such efforts are to be successful, they clearly require accurate cholesterol test results.

The Subcommittee on Investigations and Oversight of the House Committee on Science, Space, and Technology asked GAO to review several topics related to NCEP. Accordingly, this report addresses the following evaluation questions: (1) How is cholesterol measured? (2) What is known about the accuracy and precision of cholesterol measurement techniques? (3) What factors influence cholesterol levels? (4) What is the potential effect of uncertain measurement?

Background

Elevated levels of serum blood cholesterol have been shown to be positively correlated with increased rates of coronary heart disease. Certain amounts of cholesterol, however, are essential to the body, affecting the production of hormones and bile acids as well as being a structural component of cell membranes. Cholesterol is manufactured by the body and derived through the consumption of foods that contain cholesterol as well as those that are high in certain saturated fats.

The NCEP adult guidelines emphasize classification and treatment decisions based on a person's risk status, which is defined by serum cholesterol levels (including total, high-density lipoprotein (HDL) and low-density lipoprotein (LDL) cholesterol) in conjunction with other coronary heart disease risk factors (such as high blood pressure or a family history of heart disease). Cholesterol measurement plays a central role in the classification of individuals into risk categories (desirable, borderline high, and high) and in monitoring the progress of patients being treated. The goal for treatment is to reduce LDL cholesterol, using diet as a first step and then cholesterol-lowering drugs if diet is not successful.

Although national data indicate that cholesterol levels for the U.S. population have declined since the early 1960's, the average total serum cholesterol for adults is currently about 205 mg/dL (slightly above NCEP's borderline-high category). It is estimated that 29 percent of American adults—52 million people—are candidates for dietary therapy. Of this group, 12.7 million are considered to need drug therapy, often a lifelong proposition.

An NCEP panel of experts in 1988 found considerable inaccuracy in cholesterol testing in the United States. They and a subsequent panel in 1990 made recommendations about how cholesterol measurement could be standardized and improved. They recommended that two separate cholesterol measurements be averaged together to assess an individual's level, with a further test to be conducted if the first two varied substantially. The panels also established the goal that by 1992 a single total cholesterol measurement should be accurate within ±8.9 percent. The Health Care Financing Administration (HCFA) has also established testing requirements for total cholesterol (±10 percent) and HDL cholesterol (±30 percent).

To address the questions outlined above, GAO identified relevant scientific literature published largely since 1988, integrated findings across studies, and interviewed measurement experts who work in government agencies, private industry, universities, and clinical laboratories.

Results in Brief

NCEP has encouraged Americans to know their cholesterol number, and in fact nearly two thirds of all adults have had a cholesterol test in the past 5 years. Instrument measurement error and day-to-day variations from biological and behavioral factors make it highly unlikely that individuals can "know" their cholesterol levels based on a single measurement. Cholesterol levels should be viewed in terms of ranges rather than as absolute fixed numbers. It is important that individuals and physicians be aware of cholesterol measurement variability and that decisions to classify patients and initiate treatment be based on the average of multiple measurements and assessment of other risk factors, as recommended by the NCEP guidelines. This is particularly important when measured cholesterol levels are around the cutpoints that differentiate risk categories and may lead to recommendations for treatment with drugs.

Some progress has been made in improving analytical accuracy in cholesterol measurement, with the development of better methods and materials in recent years. Yet, cholesterol continues to be difficult to measure with accuracy and consistency across the broad range of devices and settings in which it is analyzed. Studies show that under controlled conditions, particularly research, clinical, and hospital laboratories, measurement is reasonably accurate and precise. Considerably less is known, though, about the performance of cholesterol measurement in other settings, such as physicians' office laboratories and public health screenings. Since no overall evaluation of different instruments and laboratories has been conducted, it is impossible to know whether the accuracy goals established for total and HDL cholesterol have been or could be met.

Even if a laboratory could provide reasonably accurate and precise test results, biological and behavioral factors such as diet, exercise, and illness cause an individual's cholesterol level to vary. It has been estimated that such factors may account for up to 65 percent of total variation. Studies have documented that some individuals' cholesterol levels can vary dramatically from week to week while others' remain relatively constant. Although some biological variation can be controlled for, by having individuals maintain their weight and diet for a modest period prior to measurement, many factors cannot be controlled.

Principal Findings

Measurement Methods and Analyzers

Currently, over 40 manufacturers have as many as 160 device systems on the market that use different technologies and chemical formulations to conduct cholesterol tests in different settings, making it difficult to standardize measurement. Although HCFA has registered over 150,000 U.S. laboratories that conduct medical tests, GAO could not ascertain the number of laboratories that do cholesterol tests or the number of tests that are done each year. Under the requirements of the Clinical Laboratory Improvement Amendments of 1988, HCFA has recently begun conducting laboratory inspections to assess quality control procedures and test results on all medical equipment, including cholesterol testing.

Accuracy and Precision

A process to assess and improve cholesterol measurement was established under the National Reference System for Cholesterol. Rather than require that all laboratories use the same devices and test methods, emphasis is directed toward having test results consistent with accepted accuracy standards. The Centers for Disease Control and Prevention and the National Institute of Standards and Technology have developed reference methods as well as quality control testing materials that some device manufacturers and clinical laboratories have used to assess cholesterol measurement accuracy. In addition, laboratories can participate in proficiency testing programs.

Survey data from the College of American Pathologists indicate that laboratory measurement precision for total cholesterol has improved from about 25 to 6 percent error. While several large collaborative studies of selected clinical laboratories have found that accuracy was good for patients' specimens, measurement error problems occurred when accuracy was evaluated using processed quality control materials. Because such materials behave differently from fresh patient samples and are an important component of proficiency testing programs, problems with them will severely hamper both standardization and government monitoring efforts.

Studies of desk-top analyzers have found accuracy problems for total and HDL measurements. Several devices did not meet established goals for accuracy, and estimated misclassification rates for some devices ranged from 17 to nearly 50 percent. Currently, the NCEP guidelines place a great deal of emphasis on the importance of HDL and LDL cholesterol as risk factors, which are considerably more difficult to measure than total cholesterol. LDL is usually calculated with a formula that uses measures of total cholesterol, HDL cholesterol, and triglycerides. Because the formula relies on the accuracy of these other measures, LDL measurement error can be greatly compounded.

Factors That Influence Cholesterol Levels

Some variation in an individual's total, HDL, and LDL cholesterol is normal and to be expected. A recent synthesis of several studies found that the average biological variation of total cholesterol is 6.1 percent, HDL cholesterol 7.4 percent, and LDL cholesterol 9.5 percent. Biological variation stems from behavioral factors such as diet, exercise, and alcohol consumption and clinical factors such as illness, medications, and pregnancy. Changes in the consumption of saturated fats and cholesterol raise or lower serum cholesterol levels, although individuals tend to respond quite differently to changes in diet. The extent of the effect on cholesterol levels varies depending on the amount of food intake and exercise and biological factors.

In addition, differences in the way blood specimens are collected and handled can have different results. Recent studies, for example, have reported that capillary (finger-stick) samples are more variable than venous samples, and researchers have called for more-standardized capillary collection procedures. This finding is important because capillary specimens are taken in screening settings and are used in recently approved and marketed home test kits.

Potential Effect of Inaccurate Measurements

The total error associated with analytical and biological variability can have important consequences. If, for example, the total error is assumed to be 16 percent (equivalent to the sum of the NCEP goal for analytical variability plus the average biological variability derived from a synthesis of existing studies), then a single measurement of total cholesterol with a known value of 240 mg/dL could be expected to range from 201 to 279 mg/dL. Similarly, a single measurement of HDL cholesterol with a known value of 35 mg/dL could range from 24 to 46 mg/dL based on analytical and biological variability. Multiple measurements narrow the variability; however, some variability cannot be reduced since many factors that affect cholesterol measurement cannot be controlled.

In a worst-case scenario, two types of diagnostic errors could occur if physicians do not account for measurement problems and base classification and treatment decisions on only a single measurement. A false-positive error could result in the treatment of individuals with drugs who in fact had desirable cholesterol levels. A false-negative error could result in incorrectly reassuring an individual that his or her cholesterol level was desirable. The potential for misclassification would be greatest for those who are near a high-risk cutpoint.

Recommendations

GAO is making no recommendations in this report.

Agency Comments

Officials from the Department of Health and Human Services reviewed a draft of this report and provided written comments (see appendix I). GAO incorporated many of the technical comments they provided in the text where appropriate. Overall, they believed that the state of cholesterol accuracy across the country is better than what is reflected in the draft report. However, they also acknowledged the need for better standardization materials to assess accuracy.

Contents

Contents

Abbreviations

AHA	American Heart Association
CAP	College of American Pathologists
CDC	Centers for Disease Control and Prevention
FDA	Food and Drug Administration
GAO	General Accounting Office
HCFA	Health Care Financing Administration
HDL	High-density lipoprotein
HHS	Department of Health and Human Services
LDL	Low-density lipoprotein
LSP	Laboratory Standardization Panel
NCEP	National Cholesterol Education Program
NHANES III	National Health and Nutrition Examination Survey
NHLBI	National Heart, Lung, and Blood Institute
NIH	National Institutes of Health
NIST	National Institute of Standards and Technology
NRS/CHOL	National Reference System for Cholesterol
VA	Veterans Affairs
VLDL	Very-low-density lipoprotein

Chapter 1

Introduction

The National Institutes of Health (NIH) emphasizes lowering cholesterol as an important aspect of preventing coronary heart disease. In 1985, NIH's National Heart, Lung, and Blood Institute (NHLBI) initiated the National Cholesterol Education Program (NCEP), which has undertaken a major effort to encourage individuals to measure, track, and reduce their cholesterol levels (notably total and low-density lipoprotein (LDL) cholestrol) with the objective of reducing mortality and morbidity from coronary heart disease. The focus on cholesterol reduction has come at a time when increased emphasis has also been given to modifying other risk factors associated with heart disease such as cigarette smoking and hypertension.

One aspect of the efforts to broaden awareness of cholesterol as a risk factor has been to encourage individuals to "know your cholesterol number." This advice has been heeded by the public. According to data compiled by the Centers for Disease Control and Prevention (CDC) from 47 states and the District of Columbia, the percentage of adults who reported having had their total cholesterol checked in the past 5 years ranged from 56 percent in New Mexico to 71 percent in Connecticut (median across the states sampled: 64 percent). The percentage of persons who had been told their cholesterol is high by a health professional ranged from 14 percent in New Mexico to 21 percent in Michigan (median across the states sampled: 17 percent).[1]

For a widespread cholesterol-lowering campaign to be credible, however, test results must be accurate across the diverse devices and settings in which cholesterol is measured. This is because the guidelines for treating elevated cholesterol are predicated on test results that place an individual into different risk categories. In this report, we discuss what is known about the accuracy of cholesterol testing, including how it is measured, factors that hinder accurate measurements, and efforts to improve the accuracy of cholesterol tests.

Background

Coronary heart disease is one of the leading causes of death for both men and women in the United States, accounting for 478,530 deaths in 1991, according to the American Heart Association (AHA). Of these deaths, 52 percent were men and 48 percent were women. Approximately 6.3 million people alive today in the United States have a history of heart attack, chest pain, or both; of this group, 44 percent are 60 years of age and older, 25 percent are 40 to 59 years old, and 31 percent are younger than 40.

---

[1]These figures were collected in 1991 through CDC's Behavioral Risk Factor State Survey.

Further, 1.5 million Americans are expected to suffer a heart attack in 1994. The death rate from heart attack in the United States, however, declined 32 percent between 1981 and 1991.[2] Reasons cited as contributing to this decline include improved medical care of patients and preventive measures in the population.[3]

AHA estimates that total costs associated with coronary heart disease are $56.3 billion per year. Of this figure, $37.2 billion is spent on hospital and nursing home services, $8.7 billion on physicians and nurses services, and $2.4 billion on drugs. Lost output associated with heart disease is valued at $8 billion.[4]

Because of the large sums being spent on treatment, to say nothing of the attendant psychological and social costs, prevention has been emphasized. NHLBI has established several education programs, such as NCEP, to inform the public about different risk factors associated with coronary heart disease and to provide guidelines for reducing risks that are modifiable. Other programs include the National High Blood Pressure Education Program, which began in 1972; the Smoking Education Program (1985); and the Obesity Education Initiative (1991).

NCEP Guidelines

A consensus development conference of scientific experts brought together by NIH in 1984 concluded that the risk of coronary heart disease is positively related to increased levels of serum cholesterol and that lowering elevated cholesterol levels can reduce coronary heart disease risk for individuals. The conference experts based their conclusions on the accumulated evidence from a large body of epidemiological, animal, metabolic, and clinical studies. Of major importance was the results of the Lipid Research Clinics Coronary Primary Prevention Trial, a large randomized study completed in 1984 that provided evidence that treatment to lower high cholesterol levels in patients can reduce the risk of coronary heart disease.[5] The conference experts further recommended

---

[2]American Heart Association, Heart and Stroke Facts: 1994 Statistical Supplement (Dallas, Texas: 1993), p. 10.

[3]Committee on Diet and Health, National Research Council, Diet and Health: Implications for Reducing Chronic Disease Risk (Washington, D.C.: 1989).

[4]American Heart Association, p. 22.

[5]Funded by NIH, the Lipid Research Clinics trial studied 3,806 middle-aged men with high serum cholesterol levels (mean baseline total cholesterol of 280 mg/dL) and no known symptoms of coronary heart disease. After 7.4 years of follow-up, the incidence of coronary heart disease events (myocardial infarction and sudden cardiac death) was reported to be 7 percent for those in the drug treatment group (cholestyramine) compared to 8.6 percent for those in the placebo group, a 19-percent relative risk reduction (significant at $p < .05$).

plans for establishing the National Cholesterol Education Program, which began in 1985.

NCEP has convened several expert panels and issued a series of guidelines, reports, and educational materials on the management and control of cholesterol for health care professionals and the general public. The program emphasizes two parallel approaches: (1) a clinical approach that attempts to identify and treat individuals who are at high risk and (2) a broader population approach that aims to reduce cholesterol levels for the entire population.

Clinical guidelines for reducing elevated cholesterol levels in adults over 20 years of age were first issued by the Adult Treatment Panel in 1987 and were subsequently updated in a second expert panel report in 1993. These guidelines cover the classification of cholesterol, patient evaluation, and dietary and drug treatments. In 1990, NCEP outlined population strategies to lower total and LDL cholesterol by encouraging all Americans to be aware that elevated cholesterol is a potential risk factor for coronary heart disease, have their cholesterol measured at regular intervals, and modify their diet. NCEP published another report in 1991 that addressed cholesterol issues in children and adolescents. It emphasized strategies for encouraging the nation's youths to reduce their intake of saturated fat and cholesterol as well as identifying and treating those whose high serum cholesterol levels put them at increased risk for heart disease as adults. The recommendations made in NCEP reports are disseminated and implemented through 40 agencies, such as AHA, that conduct health education and information activities.

Adult Treatment Guidelines

The current NCEP adult treatment guidelines emphasize classification and treatment decisions based on a person's risk status, which is defined not only by serum cholesterol levels (including total cholesterol and its low-density lipoprotein (LDL) and high-density lipoprotein (HDL) components) but also by what other coronary risk factors are present. Those with symptoms of coronary heart disease or with at least two other coronary heart disease risk factors are considered candidates for more intensive treatment.

Positive risk factors are

- Hypertension (>140/90 mm Hg, or on antihypertensive medication)
- Current cigarette smoking

- Diabetes
- Family history of myocardial infarction or sudden death before age 55 in father or male sibling, before age 65 in mother or female sibling
- Age: male >45 years of age or female >55 years of age or postmenopausal and not on estrogen replacement therapy
- Low HDL cholesterol (<35 mg/dL)

A negative risk factor is

- HDL cholesterol >60 mg/dL.[6]

The guidelines recommend that all adults have their total cholesterol measured at least once every 5 years and that HDL cholesterol be measured at the same time. As shown in figure 1.1, adults without evidence of existing coronary heart disease are classified initially into three levels based on total cholesterol levels—desirable (below (<) 200 mg/dL), borderline high (200-239 mg/dL), and high (equal to or above (>) 240 mg/dL). An HDL cholesterol level of less than 35 mg/dL is considered low and a contributing risk factor for coronary heart disease. The cutpoints for total cholesterol are based largely on epidemiological data that have shown that the risk of heart disease increases as cholesterol levels rise. For example, in 361,000 men screened for the Multiple Risk Factor Intervention Trial, those at or above the 90th percentile of total cholesterol, about 263 mg/dL, had a four times greater risk of death from coronary heart disease than those in the bottom 20 percent (< 182 mg/dL).[7]

---

[6]An HDL cholesterol level greater than or equal to 60 mg/dL is considered to be a negative risk factor because at this level it appears to have a protective effect against coronary heart disease. Our source for positive and negative risk factors is "Second Report of the Expert Panel on Detection, Evaluation, and Treatment of High Blood Cholesterol in Adults," National Cholesterol Education Program, Bethesda, Maryland, 1993.

[7]M. J. Martin et al., "Serum Cholesterol, Blood Pressure, and Mortality: Implications from a Cohort of 361,662 Men," Lancet, 2 (1986), 933-36.

Figure 1.1: Primary Prevention in Adults Without Evidence of Coronary Heart Disease: Total and HDL Cholesterol

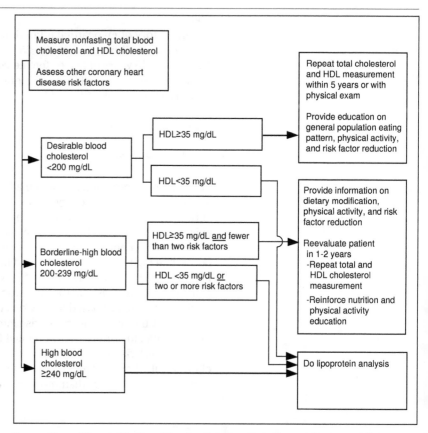

Source: "Second Report of the Expert Panel on Detection, Evaluation, and Treatment of High Blood Cholesterol in Adults," National Cholesterol Education Program, Bethesda, Maryland, 1993.

As indicated in figure 1.1, individuals are recommended for a followup lipoprotein analysis depending on an assessment of their total cholesterol and HDL cholesterol levels in conjunction with the presence or absence of other coronary heart disease risk factors. Thus, those who would be candidates for a subsequent lipoprotein analysis include individuals with (1) high total cholesterol (≥240 mg/dL), (2) borderline-high cholesterol (200-239 mg/dL) and low HDL cholesterol (<35 mg/dL), or (3) borderline-high cholesterol (200-239 mg/dL), higher HDL cholesterol (>35 mg/dL), and two or more risk factors.

Lipoprotein analysis includes measurement of fasting levels of total cholesterol, HDL cholesterol, and triglycerides and the calculation of LDL cholesterol, which is derived by a mathematical formula. The subsequent classification of adults based on LDL cholesterol levels is shown in figure 1.2. NCEP also classifies LDL cholesterol into three levels—desirable (<130 mg/dL), borderline-high risk (130-159 mg/dL), and high risk (>160 mg/dL). Decisions for beginning diet or drug treatment are then based on these levels in combination with other risk factors (see table 1.1). Thus, candidates for diet therapy without known symptoms of coronary heart disease include those with high LDL cholesterol (>160 mg/dL) or those with borderline-high LDL cholesterol (130-159 mg/dL) plus two or more risk factors.

Figure 1.2: Primary Prevention in Adults Without Evidence of Coronary Heart Disease: LDL Cholesterol

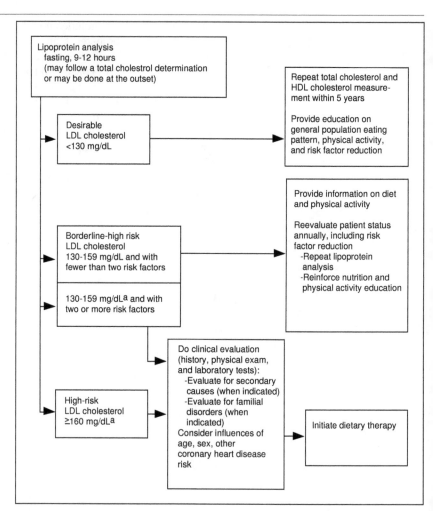

[a]On the basis of the average of two determinations. If the first two LDL cholesterol tests differ by more than 30 mg/dL, a third test should be obtained within 1 to 8 weeks, and the average value of the three tests should be used.

Source: "Second Report of the Expert Panel on Detection, Evaluation, and Treatment of High Blood Cholesterol in Adults," National Cholesterol Education Program, Bethesda, Maryland, 1993.

Table 1.1: Treatment Recommendations Based on LDL Cholesterol[a]

Treatment	With or without coronary heart disease	LDL level to begin treatment	LDL goal of treatment
Dietary	Without and fewer than two risk factors	≥160	<160
	Without and two or more risk factors	≤130	<130
	With	>100	≤100
Drug	Without and fewer than two risk factors	≥190[b]	<160
	Without and two or more risk factors	≥160	<130
	With	≥130[c]	<100

[a]All values are in mg/dL.

[b]In men under 35 years and premenopausal women with LDL cholesterol levels 190-219 mg/dL, it is recommended that drug therapy be delayed except in high-risk patients like those with diabetes.

[c]In coronary heart disease patients with LDL cholesterol levels 100-129 mg/dL, it is recommended that the physician exercise clinical judgment in deciding whether to initiate drug treatment.

Source: "Second Report of the Expert Panel on Detection, Evaluation, and Treatment of High Blood Cholesterol in Adults," National Cholesterol Education Program, Bethesda, Maryland, 1993.

NCEP recommends diet therapy as a first line of treatment for most patients except those at particularly high risk who may warrant drug intervention immediately, such as individuals with existing coronary heart disease. NCEP's recommended step I and step II diets are designed to reduce consumption of saturated fat and cholesterol and to promote weight loss in overweight patients.[8] If diet therapy is ineffective at lowering LDL cholesterol levels, then drug treatment is advised. NCEP has developed a series of guidelines for administering different types of drugs that are available to lower cholesterol. It should be noted that initiating drug treatment commits patients to long-term therapy, which may be for the rest of their lives.

Some perspective on what these treatment categories and recommendations mean for Americans can be seen in recently collected, nationally representative data from the first phase of the National Health and Nutrition Examination Survey (NHANES III).[9] These data indicate that

[8]The step I diet includes the following conditions: saturated fat consumption of 8-10 percent of total calories, 30 percent or less of calories from total fat, and cholesterol less than 300 mg/day; the more stringent step II diet lowers saturated fat consumption to less than 7 percent of total calories and cholesterol to less than 200 mg/day.

[9]C. L. Johnson et al., "Declining Serum Total Cholesterol Levels Among U.S. Adults: The National Health and Nutrition Examination Surveys," Journal of the American Medical Association, 269 (1993), 3002-8.

the average total serum cholesterol level is 205 mg/dL for men 20 years old and older and 207 mg/dL for women 20 years old and older. As shown in figure 1.3, women tend to have lower total cholesterol levels compared to men up until the ages of 45 to 54, at which time it increases to levels above those of men. This difference may be attributed, in part, to menopause, which influences women's lipid and hormonal levels. Whether this increases women's coronary heart disease risk is not clear, according to some research. Overall, women appear to have higher HDL cholesterol levels then men do, which may also account for part of this difference.[10]

---

[10]Differences in HDL levels by gender were consistent across racial groups. In non-Hispanic blacks, men's HDL levels averaged 53 mg/dL, women's 58 mg/dL. Mexican-American men had an average HDL of 47 mg/dL and women 53 mg/dL. Non-Hispanic white men had the lowest average HDL levels (46 mg/dL) while women in this group averaged 56 mg/dL.

Figure 1.3: Total, LDL, and HDL Serum Cholesterol Levels for U.S. Adults 20 Years Old and Older

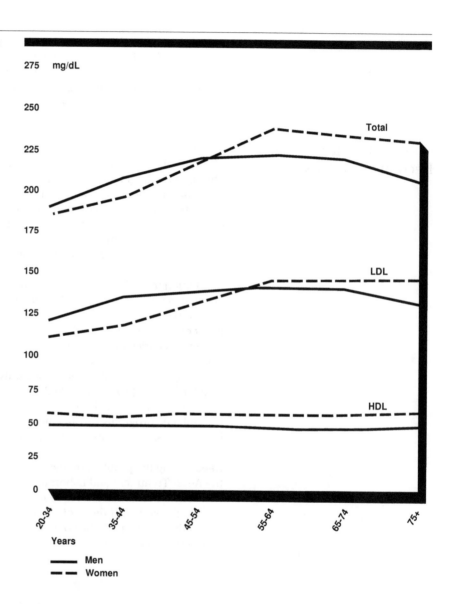

While trend data indicate that cholesterol levels have declined since the early 1960's, 52 million U.S. adults, or 29 percent, have an LDL cholesterol level that is classified as borderline-high or high according to the NCEP guidelines and that, when combined with other risk factors, makes them candidates for dietary therapy.[11] Of the 52 million adults mentioned above, about 12.7 million have cholesterol levels sufficiently elevated that they might be candidates for drug therapy (about one third of this group would be patients with coronary heart disease).

Cholesterol Measurement Recommendations

NCEP's Laboratory Standardization Panel (LSP) has issued two reports on cholesterol measurement. The first report, issued in 1988, focused attention on the importance of accurate measurements. In the report's introduction, the panel stated: "the current state of reliability of blood cholesterol measurements made in the United States suggests that considerable inaccuracy in cholesterol testing exists."[12] That report, along with press articles critical of cholesterol testing in 1987, drew attention to the need for more consistent and replicable results.

In addition to outlining the state of the art in cholesterol testing, the NCEP/LSP reports describe factors that can affect test accuracy and reliability: analytical problems (laboratory analyzer inaccuracy and imprecision) and preanalytical factors (biological variation, disease, conditions under which a sample is taken). The second report published in 1990 also contains a number of recommendations to improve laboratory testing systems. These include using only analytical systems whose standardization process is linked to the National Reference System for Cholesterol (NRS/CHOL, discussed in chapter 3), participating in external surveillance programs (proficiency testing), comparing results with other laboratories, and using quality controls to monitor analytical performance.

Recognizing the problem of measurement variability in cholesterol testing, the Adult Treatment and Laboratory Standardization Panels recommended that total and LDL cholesterol be measured on two separate occasions and averaged together. If the cholesterol results differ by 30 mg/dL or more, then a third test should be conducted and the three tests averaged together to assess an individual's cholesterol level.

---

[11]According to the government's Interagency Board for Nutrition Monitoring and Related Research, doctor-recommended diets to lower cholesterol rose 6 percent between 1983 and 1990. In 1990, 15 percent of the population followed self-prescribed diets to lower cholesterol and slightly less than 10 percent were on doctor-recommended diets. See Nutrition Monitoring in the United States: Selected Findings from the National Nutrition Monitoring and Related Research Program (Hyattsville, Md.: 1993), p. 63.

[12]Laboratory Standardization Panel, National Cholesterol Education Program, Current Status of Cholesterol Measurement in Clinical Laboratories in the United States (Bethesda, Md.: 1988), p. 1.

NCEP/LSP established the goal that a single serum total cholesterol measurement should be accurate within +8.9 percent. This goal of +8.9 percent was effective in 1992, replacing the interim goal of +14.2 percent that had been established in 1988.[13] NCEP has not previously issued goals for HDL and LDL cholesterol measurement; however, an expert panel convened by NCEP has recently developed such goals and they are expected to be published shortly.

The Clinical Laboratory Improvement Amendments of 1988 (Public Law 100-578) also mandated that the Secretary of Health and Human Services (HHS) establish performance standards such as quality control, quality assurance, and personnel regulations. HCFA testing requirements for total cholesterol, authored by CDC, stipulate a +10 percent criterion for acceptable performance for proficiency testing purposes. HCFA testing requirements for HDL cholesterol for acceptable performance on proficiency testing specimens is +30 percent of the established target value.

Although the NCEP guidelines advocate multiple measurements, there has been concern by some researchers that, in practice, physicians may not take measurement variability into account when making treatment decisions about cholesterol. Given that the NCEP classification levels for cholesterol are relatively narrow and that the average cholesterol levels for the U.S. population are in the borderline-high category at about 205 mg/dL, there is potential that patients can be misclassified. That is, measurement errors can lead to individuals with "true" levels below the high cutpoint of 240 mg/dL for total cholesterol or 160 mg/dL for LDL cholesterol being put on treatment (termed a false positive) or conversely those with "true" levels above the cutpoints not being treated (a false negative).

Objectives, Scope, and Methodology

In discussions with the requester, we agreed to focus our review of cholesterol measurement on the following evaluation questions:[14]

---

[13]The total error goal is ≤3 percent bias and <3 percent imprecision, at the 0.05 level of significance, 2-tailed test. This means that if an individual's true total cholesterol were 200 mg/dL, and the same specimen were tested 100 times, 95 of these tests should fall between 182.2 and 217.8 mg/dL. Clinical chemists use the measurement term "precision" differently from social scientists and evaluators. It is used to describe what social scientists term "reliability"—that is, whether a test or measure gives the same result on repeated trials.

[14]In a subsequent study, we will report on issues pertaining to the clinical trials evidence that supports the NCEP guidelines.

1. How is cholesterol measured? (See chapter 2.)

2. What is known about the accuracy and precision of cholesterol measurement techniques? (See chapter 3.)

3. What factors influence cholesterol levels? (See chapter 4.)

4. What is the potential effect of uncertain measurement? (See chapter 5.)

To answer these questions, we identified and reviewed relevant scientific literature published mainly since 1988 and synthesized data across studies to address these questions. We selected this period because it covered the time since the first NCEP cholesterol measurement goals were issued, permitting a benchmark by which later testing could be judged. We conducted our bibliographic search using on-line data bases of medical literature. Other sources included articles recommended by experts in the field and the bibliographies of articles published in medical and related research journals. We identified and reviewed approximately 125 books and articles relevant to cholesterol measurement in this manner.

We supplemented our review of the medical literature with interviews with a range of individuals who have expertise in the field. These included government agency officials involved with cholesterol measurement and testing issues at CDC, the Food and Drug Administration (FDA), HCFA, NIH, and the National Institute of Standards and Technology (NIST). We also interviewed manufacturers of analyzers in private industry, university researchers, and representatives of organizations that conduct proficiency testing for laboratories. In order to have a better understanding of the testing process, we visited a major hospital laboratory facility to discuss quality control issues and challenges facing practitioners. We also visited a major manufacturer of analyzers to learn more about the production process (quality control procedures, analyzer calibration, potential sources of inaccuracy) as well as industry concerns about the accuracy and precision of cholesterol testing. We did not, however, independently evaluate laboratory performance in any of the different settings where cholesterol tests are conducted across the country.

Chapter 2

Cholesterol Measurement: Methods, Settings, and Analyzers

In this chapter, we answer the first evaluation question: How is cholesterol measured? The discussion begins with an overview of cholesterol's role in the body and analyzes how total cholesterol, HDL, LDL, apolipoproteins, and triglycerides are measured, focusing on laboratory techniques. We also describe the range of settings where cholesterol testing is done and review the type of analyzers for sale in the U.S. market.

Cholesterol measurement focuses mainly on determining levels of total, HDL, and LDL cholesterol. Triglyceride levels are also included in lipid profiles. Cholesterol is commonly tested in a variety of settings ranging from large health fairs to more specialized clinical laboratories. No national data are available on the number of laboratories that conduct cholesterol tests, the number of cholesterol testing devices in use in laboratories, or the number of such tests that are done each year. The universe of U.S. laboratories that conduct different types of medical tests is large, however, with some 154,403 having registered with HCFA by October 1993. While HCFA data indicate that physicians' offices predominate in the testing arena, the distribution of cholesterol tests is not ascertainable from these data. Test results may be less accurate from such settings because of the type of devices used and less staff expertise in conducting tests.

In addition to the broad range of settings where measurements are conducted, a large number of analyzers on the market measure cholesterol (45 manufacturers make 166 test systems that measure total cholesterol). Because some of these analyzers are used with different chemical formulations to conduct cholesterol tests, standardizing measurements is a complex task (a topic taken up in chapter 3). A related measurement issue is the use of enzymatic materials in cholesterol analyzers. While enzymatic materials have permitted improvements in ease of use, they are difficult to characterize chemically because they may deteriorate or vary with time, introducing potential measurement inaccuracy.

Cholesterol's Role in the Body

While considerable attention has been given to the negative consequences of elevated total and LDL cholesterol levels, cholesterol is essential to body processes, affecting the production of steroid hormones and bile acids as well as being a structural component of cellular membranes. Cholesterol is a fat-like substance (lipid) manufactured by the body and is also ingested directly through foods such as eggs, which contain cholesterol. In addition, certain saturated fats raise the blood cholesterol level more than any other nutrient component in the diet. If you eat a "standard" American diet, two thirds of the cholesterol in your body is manufactured by your cells—the remainder is derived from your diet. Thus, an elevated cholesterol level may be the result of a diet heavy in saturated fat and cholesterol; it is also possible that the liver is manufacturing high levels of cholesterol and triglyceride or that cholesterol is being removed too slowly from the body.

Cholesterol is transported in blood plasma through lipoproteins. The three major classes of lipoproteins include LDL (containing 60 to 70 percent of the total serum cholesterol), HDL (containing 20 to 30 percent of the total serum cholesterol), and VLDL (very low density lipoproteins, which are precursors of LDL and contain 10 to 15 percent of the total serum cholesterol). Triglycerides are also an important lipid in the blood and are usually measured in conjunction with cholesterol values. More recently, increased scientific attention has been given to the apolipoprotein "families," the subcomponents that make up these types of cholesterol, because they may be better predictors of certain risks associated with coronary heart disease such as degenerative changes in arterial walls. At present, however, research on this topic continues to be developed and tests for measuring apolipoproteins cannot be done in most laboratories.

Total Cholesterol Measurement

Of the different cholesterol types, total cholesterol is the best understood and documented, in large part because of work done at NIST and CDC to standardize measurement techniques (see chapter 3). In general laboratory practice, total cholesterol measurement is commonly accomplished by several different enzymatic methods using a variety of reagent materials.[1] The various procedures used make standardization of technique across different reagents and instrument configurations difficult.

HDL Cholesterol Measurement

HDL cholesterol, sometimes referred to as the "good" cholesterol, has become recognized as an important coronary heart disease risk factor. HDL is the smallest in size of the lipoproteins and its major subcomponents are apo AI, or apolipoproteins AI, and apo AII. Because a validated reference method has not been developed for HDL measurement, a patient specimen comparison with CDC's procedure is considered the best means to assess accuracy. HDL cholesterol is difficult to measure accurately, however, and current criteria under the Clinical Laboratory Improvement Amendments

---

[1]For discussion of different total cholesterol measurement methods, see J. D. Artiss et al., "Measurement of Cholesterol Concentration," in Methods for Clinical Laboratory Measurement of Lipid and Lipoprotein Risk Factors, N. Rifai and G. R. Warnick (eds.) (Washington, D.C.: AACC Press, 1991), pp. 33-50.

of 1988 for acceptable laboratory performance are that a sample must be +30 percent of a test target value, a relatively broad range even with lower HDL values. CDC officials we interviewed pointed out that considerable scientific work remains before HDL measurement accuracy is as well understood as total cholesterol currently is. This would include developing accurate reference materials that could be used to evaluate how well analyzers are measuring HDL cholesterol.

LDL Cholesterol Measurement

Low-density lipoprotein cholesterol, sometimes referred to as the "bad" cholesterol, is considered to be the principal fraction that causes plaque to build up on arterial walls. No error standards for LDL cholesterol measurement have been established under the Clinical Laboratory Improvement Amendments of 1988 or NCEP, although NCEP expects to issue such standards shortly. Direct measurement of LDL cholesterol can be accomplished through ultracentrifugation methods; however, such methods are expensive and time consuming to conduct and therefore not generally available in most cholesterol test settings.[2]

In practice, LDL cholesterol is calculated from other laboratory measurements using the Friedewald formula: LDL = total cholesterol − HDL − (triglycerides/5). Among the several limitations to the Friedewald formula is that a patient should be fasting when the specimen is taken. The formula cannot be used for individuals with extremely high triglyceride levels (400 mg/dL and above) and several rare lipid conditions. The most crucial constraint related to the Friedewald formula is that because it relies heavily on the accuracy and precision of total cholesterol, HDL, and total triglycerides, potential measurement error is compounded.

Triglycerides

Triglyceride levels are usually measured along with lipoprotein levels because they are considered an important health indicator for certain diseases, including coronary heart disease in some patients. Triglycerides are also important to measure because they are used to calculate LDL cholesterol with the Friedewald equation. Enzymatic methods are used to analyze triglyceride levels, although the calibration of such methods is not linked to a validated definitive or reference method. As with HDL and LDL cholesterol, the CDC method (in this case, a chemical chromatropic acid method) is considered the best means for comparing accuracy. Current criteria under the 1988 amendments for acceptable laboratory

---

[2]There has been one recent advance in LDL measurement. A private company, Genzyme, has introduced a direct LDL cholesterol measure that permits testing to be done in a nonfasting state. This method could eliminate the need for multiple tests as well as provide added patient convenience.

performance are that a sample must be ±25 percent of a proficiency test target value.

Apolipoprotein Measurement

As analytical capabilities have increased, attention has also turned to the apolipoproteins, which make up HDL and LDL cholesterol. This interest is linked to finding other relevant markers for coronary heart disease risk. For example, recent research has focused on apolipoprotein B-100 (apo B), which is an integral component of four major lipoproteins—LDL, VLDL, intermediate density lipoprotein, and lipoprotein(a)—and apo AI, the major protein component of HDL. At present, several assay methods are available to measure different apolipoprotein components; however, these methods have not yet been standardized. Another practical difficulty in using these apolipoproteins is that a comprehensive, statistically sound study has not yet been undertaken that can be used as a comparative reference base.

The Use of Ratios to Determine Coronary Heart Disease Risk

One issue addressed in the medical literature concerns combining cholesterol levels to determine a ratio that is used to evaluate a patient's risk of developing coronary heart disease—for example, a total cholesterol or LDL to HDL ratio. In some instances, individuals are advised to achieve a specific ratio as an indicator of an acceptable cholesterol level. Such ratios have been useful estimators of coronary heart disease risk in some population studies; however, NCEP emphasizes that HDL and LDL cholesterol levels are independent risk factors with different determinants and should not be combined for clinical decisionmaking.

Test Settings

Widespread awareness of elevated total cholesterol levels as a potential coronary heart disease risk factor has led to patient testing in a variety of settings. These range from traditional clinical settings (hospitals, physician office laboratories) to mass screenings (such as health fairs). No national data are available on the number of laboratories that conduct cholesterol tests, the number of cholesterol testing devices in use in laboratories, or the number of such tests that are done each year.

The Clinical Laboratory Improvement Amendments of 1988 changed federal regulation of laboratories and expanded federal oversight to virtually all testing laboratories in the nation. The amendments required all laboratories to register with HCFA and established testing and quality control standards, including provisions for conducting inspections to ensure that laboratories are maintaining proper controls and records. In implementing the act, the Secretary of HHS established three categories of laboratory tests: (1) simple tests, (2) tests of moderate complexity, and (3) tests of high complexity. Waivers are given to laboratories that conduct only simple tests such as dipstick or tablet reagent urinalysis. Cholesterol tests are in the moderate complexity group, meaning that laboratories that perform such tests should comply with regulations under the amendments for personnel standards, quality control, and proficiency testing (these tests evaluate accuracy and precision using quality control materials).

As of October 1993, 154,403 laboratory facilities in the United States had registered with HCFA. HCFA officials estimate that there may be as many as 50,000 additional laboratories that should have registered with HCFA but have not, making it impossible to determine the universe of such facilities. Table 2.1 categorizes laboratories that had registered with HCFA. Of the registered laboratories, the majority, 90,673 (58.7 percent), are located in physicians' offices.

Table 2.1: Types of Laboratories Registered With HCFA[a]

Type of laboratory	Number	Percent
Physician's office	90,673	58.7%
Nursing facility	11,872	7.7
Hospital	8,922	5.8
Community clinic	7,063	4.6
Independent	6,302	4.1
Home health agency	5,083	3.3
Other practitioner	2,714	1.8
Ancillary testing site in health care facility	2,115	1.4
End-stage renal disease dialysis facility	1,614	1.0
Industrial	1,154	0.7
Ambulatory surgical center	1,000	0.6
Health maintenance organization	979	0.6
School or student health service	834	0.5
Mobile unit	603	0.4
Intensive care facility	516	0.3
Health fair	489	0.3
Pharmacy	304	0.2
Hospice	301	0.2
Blood bank	284	0.2
Tissue bank or repository	77	0
Comprehensive outpatient rehabilitation facility	66	0
Insurance	43	0
Other	10,380	6.7
Unknown	1,015	0.7
Total	**154,403**	**100.0%**

[a]That is, laboratories regulated under Public Law 100-578. These classifications are based on how laboratories classified themselves when surveyed by HCFA.

Source: Health Care Financing Administration, Baltimore, Maryland, October 1993.

Oversight of the laboratories listed in table 2.1 varies, depending on the level of tests performed and several factors. A large number, 67,000, conduct only tests that are not medically complex and are therefore exempt from regulation; 6,500 are accredited by a state agency; 24,000 are accredited by nongovernment proficiency testing groups; 16,000 conduct microscopic tests under HCFA oversight. HCFA coordinates biannual, on-site inspections by state agencies and HCFA regional office laboratory consultants for the remaining 41,000 laboratories.

HCFA expects to have 180 state agency surveyors nationwide who will work under 10 different HCFA regional offices.[3] On-site inspections will consist of examining a sample of laboratory tests based on volume, specialties, clients, and the number of shifts over which equipment is used. In their inspections, surveyors will look at the following five areas: patient test management and organization, results of proficiency tests, personnel qualifications, quality assurance procedures, and use of daily quality controls.

HCFA staff began laboratory inspections under the 1988 amendments in September 1992 and they hope to have the first cycle of visits and certifications completed by March 1995. The initial emphasis of inspections has been to educate and inform laboratory personnel about pertinent regulations. HCFA staff responsible for overseeing laboratory inspections stated that of the 6,200 survey visits that had been made by August 1993, 500 laboratories were found to have major deficiencies (the nature of these problems was not specified).

HCFA survey and certification officials and NCEP have expressed concern that cholesterol testing in physicians' offices or screening settings may differ from that done in clinical and research settings. For instance, clinical laboratories or hospitals may be more likely to have well-established quality control programs and large analyzers while physicians' offices or health fairs may be limited to less reliable desk-top analyzers and less expertise in conducting tests and maintaining analyzers (see the discussion of analyzer types in chapter 3). HCFA staff stated that physicians' offices often send specimens for HDL and LDL tests to larger laboratories, which have the capability to do these tests.

While enforcement under the 1988 amendments is relatively new, each of the groups most affected—HCFA, laboratory personnel, and proficiency testing service providers—views it differently. HCFA officials noted from their experience overseeing laboratories that the traditionally unregulated segment of the medical testing market, physicians' office laboratories, sees the regulations as a burden and an added cost. In contrast, laboratories that have maintained a high-quality testing program believe the regulations represent minimum standards for running a quality testing program. Proficiency testing service providers have had to confront problems with the quality control materials they use to assess and transfer accuracy

---

[3]When the Clinical Laboratory Improvement Amendments of 1988 was enacted, it was expected that the various agency regulatory activities would be fully implemented by 1991. However, the development of regulations was complex and time consuming, thus delaying the program start-up until 1992.

among laboratories, attempting to balance the limits of these materials with how they are used to judge laboratory performance. All agree, however, that meeting the standards adds to the cost of testing.

There are also several types of nonmedical settings in which testing is routinely undertaken: health fairs, shopping malls, and the workplace. In some cases, only a small amount of blood taken from the finger (capillary source) is used to conduct such a cholesterol analysis. These testing environments are subject to a variety of potential problems, however: poorly trained personnel taking samples, inappropriate patient preparation, incorrect specimen collection, or improperly calibrated analyzers. There is also concern that in nonmedical settings individuals may be given test results without proper interpretation. An additional concern is that those who need to be referred for further medical consultation or a more detailed cholesterol profile may not receive that advice.

Cholesterol Analyzers

FDA reviews and clears diagnostic devices, including those that measure cholesterol. Following section 510(k) of the Food, Drug, and Cosmetic Act of 1976, device manufacturers must notify FDA that they intend to market a device. FDA then determines whether the device is accurate, safe, effective, and substantially equivalent to a legally marketed "predicate" device—that is, one that was on the market when this law was passed. If the agency determines that a device does not meet 510(k) guidelines and deems it not substantially equivalent, then it must be reviewed as a new product. According to agency officials, FDA's review of cholesterol measurement devices takes into consideration information provided by manufacturers on intended use, test type and methodologies, performance characteristics (derived from actual assays), analytical performance for 40 normal and 40 abnormal specimens across the range of cholesterol levels, and label wording (intended use statement and conditions).

FDA officials indicated that the agency requests that cholesterol device manufacturers compare their analyzers to the accuracy and precision methods of the National Reference Method Laboratory Network for total cholesterol measurement (see chapter 3). However, FDA does not formally require that analyzers be "traceable" to this method because there are devices on the market that have not established "traceability" to the reference method (traceability refers to the ability of a device to closely duplicate the accuracy attained by the reference method).

CDC has compiled a list of total and HDL cholesterol analyzers currently in use. As of April 1994, there were 166 test systems (made by 45 different manufacturers) available to measure total cholesterol. For HDL cholesterol, 143 test systems, made by 41 manufacturers, have been identified. (Some manufacturers have as many as 11 "systems" that use the same technology.)

FDA-cleared cholesterol analyzers encompass three types of devices: large stationary analyzers used in clinical laboratories, desk-top analyzers, and home test kit analyzers. Desk-top analyzers can be used in a variety of settings (medical and nonmedical) to provide relatively quick cholesterol test results, whereas large analyzers are capable of performing multiple tests on many analyses for hundreds of specimens a day. The latter are usually found in large independent laboratories, hospital laboratories, and the offices of major testing organizations that serve the medical community.

The third type is a home test kit, designed for sale directly to consumers. Currently, one device, the AccuMeter (manufactured by ChemTrak) is being marketed in the United States. The approval of this device has been somewhat controversial in the clinical chemistry field because of concerns about the reliability of its measurements. Apart from possible technical problems is the related issue of whether a person may incorrectly interpret his or her cholesterol level after using the device or initiate a self-treatment program without proper medical feedback and monitoring.

Cholesterol analyzers currently on the market primarily use enzymatic methods, high-technology equipment, and computerized data processing systems. Enzymatic methods offer advantages over older chemicals because they are safer and can be used in an automated laboratory environment, both distinct improvements. Nonetheless, enzymatic methods are also considered to be difficult to characterize chemically, thus adding to the uncertainty of tests done with them. FDA draft guidelines for approving cholesterol testing devices note that because enzymatic materials may deteriorate or vary, analyses done with them may be imprecise. A related concern noted by HCFA officials is that each analyzer and reagent combination has its own "method" for measuring cholesterol, making it difficult to assess accuracy using standardized testing materials.

An additional perspective on these devices was provided by a hospital laboratory administrator who observed that the devices used in his laboratory are self-contained "black boxes" that rely heavily on computer

technology that must be regularly calibrated as part of a routine quality
control process. Unlike the older instruments these have replaced, he
noted, these newer devices are easier to use than the older systems.
However, their complexity also means that it is hard to determine whether
something may be wrong inside the device.

Chapter 3

The Accuracy of Cholesterol Measurements

In this chapter, we answer the second evaluation question: What is known about the accuracy and precision of cholesterol measurement techniques? The discussion first focuses on national accuracy goals and efforts to standardize cholesterol measures. This is followed by an analysis of recently published literature that compares test results from different settings.

Standards for cholesterol testing have evolved from the late 1980's, when NCEP first established the goal that total cholesterol measures should be accurate within ±14.2 percent. By 1992, NCEP lowered its total cholesterol measurement goal to ±8.9 percent. HCFA established a similar total cholesterol goal (±10 percent) as well as the goal that HDL cholesterol tests should be within ±30 percent of its correct value, when judged by quality control testing. To date, an LDL cholesterol measurement goal has not been established, although one is expected soon.

Evaluating the extent to which laboratories across the country are providing medical personnel and patients with accurate total cholesterol test results is difficult. While an accepted national reference system exists, and network laboratories can provide traceability to an accuracy standard, participation by laboratories has been limited particularly to clinical and research settings. Additional information is collected through proficiency testing surveys that indicate that laboratory precision has improved over time but, again, the number of participating laboratories is small. The lack of information on accuracy in actual laboratory settings makes it impossible to know whether the goals established for total and HDL cholesterol measurement are being met and how well LDL cholesterol is being measured. Because these test results are key to making treatment decisions in NCEP guidelines, such data are arguably important.

Two collaborative research efforts, one by the College of American Pathologists (CAP) and CDC and the other by Veterans Affairs (VA) and CDC, highlight weaknesses of the current system of monitoring cholesterol laboratory tests. The reliance on processed quality control materials for evaluating analyzer accuracy was found to be problematic because of what are termed matrix effects. Processed materials tend to act differently from fresh serum samples on many instrument reagent systems and produce different test results. The studies found that total cholesterol tests done on fresh serum samples in a select group of clinical settings met NCEP accuracy standards whereas with processed control materials, there was greater inaccuracy. Finding ways to address matrix problems is important because processed control materials are key to assessing accuracy across laboratories and serve as the basis for enforcing the Clinical Laboratory Improvement Amendments of 1988.

With regard to desk-top analyzers, there are sufficient concerns about the reported accuracy and precision of total, HDL, and LDL results provided by several devices, even when tested under optimal operating conditions, to warrant further scrutiny of their performance. Consumers should be aware of the potential uncertainty associated with test results produced by these devices, particularly in screening settings. Several studies we reviewed found misclassification rates ranging from 17 to nearly 50 percent.

One new development in the cholesterol testing arena are home test devices, which measure total cholesterol. While these may prove to be useful, questions about their precision and accuracy should not be overlooked—particularly in light of their direct availability to consumers. Broader concerns about how individuals may interpret results and what they might do with that information in terms of failing to seek out appropriate medical consultation and possible treatment are too important to be ignored.

Accuracy, Precision, and NCEP Goals

NCEP's 1990 report, Recommendations for Improving Cholesterol Measurement, established performance goals for assessing the accuracy of individual laboratory testing programs. The report recommended that by 1992 the total error associated with a single serum total cholesterol measurement should be within ± 8.9 percent (0.05, 2-tailed test). Total error is defined in terms of two main measurement components: bias and precision. Bias is the extent to which a series of test results deviate from the "true" value, within acceptable limits (≤ 3 percent according to NCEP), whereas precision refers to the consistency and reliability of repeated results within acceptable limits (≤ 3 percent according to NCEP). A cholesterol analyzer, for example, could be very precise yet inaccurate because of the poor calibration of an analyzer or the deterioration of the reagents being used. The difference between bias and precision can be illustrated with the following brief example. Suppose that a total cholesterol specimen whose "true" value is 200 mg/dL were tested 10 times on the same analyzer. If the analyzer gave a reading of 220 mg/dL each time it tested the specimen, the analysis would be biased—that is, it would be 10 percent over the "true" value. However, the analysis would be precise in that it consistently gave the same result when testing the specimen—the precision error would be zero.[1]

While test results need to be unbiased and precise, there is the question of how accurate a test need be at particular cholesterol levels. It has been suggested that greater variability may be acceptable at levels well above or below the NCEP cutpoints—for example, at total cholesterol readings of 160 mg/dL or as high as 350 mg/dL. Arguably, accuracy becomes more important near the 240 mg/dL cutpoint than at 350 mg/dL, where there is less doubt about a patient's risk category.

The National Reference System for Cholesterol

The National Reference System for Cholesterol (NRS/CHOL) grew out of work undertaken by the National Committee for Clinical Laboratory Standards in 1977 to establish an accuracy base for cholesterol testing.[2] Rather than requiring that all laboratories use the same analyzers and methods to achieve standardization, emphasis is given to having test results traceable to an accepted accuracy standard. NRS/CHOL consists of a hierarchy of approved methods and materials used to assess cholesterol measurement accuracy. These include basic measurement units and definitive methods (NIST), primary reference materials (NIST), reference methods (CDC), secondary reference materials (NIST and CDC), field methods, and patients' results.[3] These are integrated into an accuracy base that can be transferred through a national laboratory network to device manufacturers and the broad range of laboratories where cholesterol is measured.

One component of NRS/CHOL involves expertise at NIST, where the definitive method for measuring total cholesterol was developed. The definitive method assigns the "true" value to a specimen through a process in which all potential sources of inaccuracy and interference are evaluated. The definitive method uses an isotope dilution mass spectrometric technique. Because it requires special equipment and costly materials and is time-consuming, the definitive method is not considered transferable to clinical laboratories. This method is also used for the highly specialized

---

[1]Precision is often measured in laboratory tests in terms of the statistical coefficient of variation, which expresses the standard deviation as a percentage of the mean value. It is used to compare precision at different concentration levels. A method's precision varies inversely with the coefficient of variation: the lower it is, the more precise the method.

[2]The committee coordinates efforts to promote laboratory standardization among professional, industrial, and government organizations.

[3]See R. E. Vanderlinde et al., "The National Reference System for Cholesterol," Clinics in Laboratory Medicine, 9:1 (1989), 89-104.

purpose of developing and testing standard reference materials that are used by manufacturers and in other settings such as research lipid laboratories.

CDC oversees another piece of NRS/CHOL: it uses what is termed the modified Abell, Levy, Brodie, and Kendall (abbreviated Abell-Kendall) reference method for total cholesterol measurement. When the reference and definitive methods have both been used to test the same samples, the reference method's results have been shown to be about 1.5-percent higher than those of the definitive method.[4]

CDC disseminates the reference method through the National Reference Method Laboratory Network for Cholesterol Standardization. This includes nine laboratories located throughout the United States and four overseas. Because the reference method is expensive and labor intensive, it is not considered practical for use in most clinical laboratories. Consequently, it is used primarily by research laboratories and manufacturers, two settings in which closer traceability to the definitive method is essential.

The network provides a support system that would permit a laboratory or manufacturer to gauge its total cholesterol test accuracy and standardize its measurements.[5] This can be done by splitting samples with a network laboratory and comparing results. Participation in the network is relatively low when one takes into consideration the number of laboratories in the United States. In 1991, for example, 170 laboratories applied for a certificate of traceability and 58 percent passed (if a laboratory fails, it can reapply for certification). In 1992, 167 laboratories applied for a certificate of traceability and 79 percent passed.

Although participation is low, CDC officials estimate that 95 percent of the types of instrument systems most common in U.S. laboratories have been certified through the reference network as meeting NCEP standards mentioned earlier in this chapter (a list of these analyzers is published in Clinical Chemistry News). CDC representatives caution that the reference laboratories test only an analytical system for potential to meet these

---

[4]P. Ellerbe et al., "A Comparison of Results for Cholesterol in Human Serum Obtained by the Reference Method and by the Definitive Method of the National Reference System for Cholesterol," Clinical Chemistry, 36 (1990), 370-75.

[5]Criteria for standardization are a correlation coefficient with the Abell-Kendall 0.975, bias at 200 and 240 mg/dL <3 percent, overall coefficient of variation <3 percent, and average absolute bias <3 percent. Acceptable performance is documented by a dated certificate of traceability that is valid for 6 months.

standards. Day-to-day consistency in a laboratory requires rigorous quality controls that help ensure that an analyzer will perform as it is capable of performing. In other words, if an analyzer is not maintained properly, it will not provide results that are constantly accurate.[6]

Another way in which NRS/CHOL attempts to transfer accuracy to laboratories is through "quality control" substances called standard reference materials, which are the link between the definitive and reference methods and manufacturers of analyzers and reagent systems. These include CDC and NIST-produced and certified materials (which are made in stabilized, frozen, or lyophilized, or freeze-dried, forms) that are assigned target values for cholesterol using the reference or definitive methods.

Proficiency Testing Services

Proficiency testing (outside surveillance) services have an increasingly important role in efforts to achieve accuracy and standardization of clinical laboratory tests because they provide the basis for interlaboratory comparison of test results and accuracy across analyzers. Proficiency testing programs send quality control materials that participating laboratories analyze and the results are compared with a target value determined by CDC's reference method. These test results are divided into peer groupings (by instrument type), permitting laboratory staff to judge how their results compare with laboratories using the same method as well as the CDC reference method result. CAP and the American Association of Bioanalysts are two major groups involved in this work. CAP's Comprehensive Chemistry Survey has 12,000 subscribers that use its service to evaluate several different clinical chemistry tests. This service is not generally used by smaller laboratories. The American Association of Bioanalysts does similar types of proficiency testing.

National trends through 1990 in interlaboratory comparability (that is, the degree to which established test values vary from one laboratory to the next) for total cholesterol are as follows: 1949, 23.7 percent; 1969, 18.5 percent; 1980, 11.1 percent; 1983, 6.4 percent; 1986, 6.2 percent; 1990, 5.5 to 7.2 percent.[7] These data indicate that interlaboratory precision in

---

[6]Measurement accuracy can also be influenced by how a sample is collected and handled prior to analysis. This includes the use of anticoagulants and preservatives and the temperature at which a specimen is stored (0-4 degrees centigrade is recommended for up to 4 days, –70 degrees centigrade for longer periods).

[7]Figures for 1949 to 1986 were taken from the NCEP/LSP report Current Status of Blood Cholesterol Measurement in Clinical Laboratories in the United States (Bethesda, Md.: 1988), p. 10. The 1990 figures were published in the NCEP report Recommendations for Improving Cholesterol Measurement (Bethesda, Md.: 1990), p. 6.

those clinical laboratories participating in the CAP survey improved considerably from variability of about 24 percent in 1949, to 1983, when it appears to have leveled off at the 6-percent range. These differences between laboratories suggest that method and laboratory-specific biases contributed to overall inconsistency in cholesterol analyses. Another indicator of precision is consistency within individual laboratories. CAP data indicate intralaboratory precision for cholesterol measurements (where participating laboratories analyze the same quality control materials repeatedly over an extended period) improved from 4.1 percent in 1975 to 3.5 percent in 1985.

Matrix Effects

Efforts to achieve standardized, accurate cholesterol measurements through NRS/CHOL and proficiency testing programs have encountered serious problems with the use of quality control (reference) materials. These are termed "matrix" effects and arise when "cholesterol recovered from the control material matrix may not compare with that typically recovered from fresh patient specimens."[8] This is because the matrix surrounding the cholesterol quality control material interferes with the analysis, causing erroneous results (matrix effects do not arise when analyzing fresh blood samples). This is a function of instrument design, reagent composition, method employed, and the material formulation. Because these quality control materials are key to transferring accuracy and quality control in NRS/CHOL and assessing precision in proficiency testing programs, matrix effects present considerable problems. While most attention has focused on matrix effects in quality control materials used to standardize total cholesterol measures, there is also concern that HDL cholesterol control materials may be subject to these effects.

Recent interest in the problems presented by matrix effects is linked to the Clinical Laboratory Improvement Amendments of 1988, which required that proficiency testing be used to evaluate the quality of laboratory results. Matrix problems can make it impossible to assign a target value to quality control material that will apply to all routine testing methods. Industry and academic research efforts are underway to address the measurement problems associated with matrix effects but practical solutions are not yet available. Research has focused on establishing correction factors to account for the matrix error component (derived from comparisons of test results using fresh samples and quality control materials) as well as on developing new analytical systems and quality

---

[8]J. W. Ross et al., "Matrix Effects and the Accuracy of Cholesterol Analysis," Archives of Pathology and Laboratory Medicine, 117:4 (1993), 393.

control materials that can accurately measure both fresh patient and quality control materials.

CAP and CDC Collaborative Study

A recently published CAP and CDC collaborative study examined matrix effects on cholesterol tests.[9] A total of 997 laboratories that participate in the CAP survey were selected (selection method was not specified) to analyze both a freshly frozen serum pool and a lyophilized (freeze-dried) CAP chemistry quality control sample simultaneously, permitting comparisons and bias to be calculated. Laboratories that had submitted incomplete data or had results considered to be outliers (defined in this study as a pooled within-run coefficient of variation across three samples that exceeded 10 percent or a within-run bias of any sample of 25 percent or more relative to the reference method value) were excluded from the analysis.[10] Laboratories that participated in the study were drawn from CAP survey participants, which are mainly hospital laboratories. They are, thus, not representative of small independent laboratories such as those found in physicians' offices, or even hospitals. While the ability to generalize from this study is limited, the authors make several points that have important consequences for cholesterol measurement.

The CAP and CDC study classified the cholesterol analysis methods into 37 instrumentation and reagent groups. This figure indicates the range of instruments and reagent combinations that regulators must work with in attempting to achieve standardization. Across this group of instruments, they found that "26 (70%) of [the] 37 methods evaluated had statistically significant calibration bias compared with the reference method. The calibration bias of 13 methods (41%) exceeded the NCEP 3% limit for bias."[11] When the investigators adjusted the results to compensate for matrix effects, "92% to 93% of adjusted results met the NCEP 8.9% total error goal relative to the reference method due to superior interlaboratory precision of some of the biased methods."[12] For the fresh-frozen serum sample that was analyzed, test results (N = 900) had a mean bias of 0.1 percent that was nearly identical to the reference method and a coefficient of variation of 4.6 percent, the latter figure slightly exceeding the 1992 NCEP/LSP goal.

---

[9]Ross et al., p. 393.

[10]Removing outliers of this magnitude results in a distribution more normal in appearance but has the effect of reducing overall sample variation.

[11]Ross et al., p. 398.

[12]Ross et al., p. 398.

Thus, 70 percent of enzymatic methods used to measure cholesterol in the CAP and CDC study were subject to matrix effects when testing quality control material. The implication of this for NRS/CHOL is that the use of fresh human samples, such as by splitting samples with a member of the National Reference Method Laboratory Network and comparing results, may be a better means to transfer accuracy than the use of processed quality control materials. Given the number of laboratories in the nation and the limited number of National Reference Method Laboratories, this would be a difficult if not impossible task. Table 3.1 lists the 37 instrument and reagent systems and calibration bias relative to the reference method.

Table 3.1: Instrument and Reagent System-Specific Calibration Bias Relative to the Reference Method

Instrument and reagent system	Number of laboratories	Calibration bias
AM Perspective/AM	18	6.3
Olympus Demand/Technicon	7	5.3
Roche Cobas Mira/Roche	29	4.7
Kone Progress/Kone	12	4.6
AM KDA/AM	8	4.5
Baker Encore/Baker	16	3.9
Roche Cobas/Roche	7	3.8
Abbott TDX/Abbott	13	3.0
Baker Centrif/Baker	12	2.3
DuPont Dimension/DuPont	43	2.2
Gilford Impact 400/Ciba	10	2.1[a]
BMD 736, 737/BMD	51	1.8
Baxter Paramax/Paramax	46	1.5
Technicon SMAC/Technicon	17	1.2[a]
Technicon 12-60/Technicon	8	1.1[a]
IL Monarch/IL	32	1.0
Olympus 5000/Olympus	10	0.7[a]
Technicon RA-1000/Technicon	27	0.3[a]
Abbott Spectrum/Abbott	40	0.1[a]
Olympus Demand/Olympus	14	−0.1[a]
Ciba 550 Express/Ciba	10	−0.3[a]
Technicon RA-1000/Sigma	7	−0.3[a]
Technicon Chem 1/Technicon	23	−0.8[a]
DuPont aca/DuPont	18	−1.2
BMD 8700/BMD	15	−1.3[a]
AM Parallel/AM	16	−1.6
BMD 704, 705/BMD	50	−1.6

(continued)

Instrument and reagent system	Number of laboratories	Calibration bias
AM Parallel/Behring	5	−1.8
BMD 717/BMD	12	−2.0
Ektachem DT 60/Kodak	13	−2.6
Coulter Dacos/Coulter	27	−3.0
Beckman Synchron CX 4,5/Beck	6	−3.2
Abbott VP/Abbott	19	−3.2
Beckman Astra 4,8, Ideal/Beck	52	−3.2
IL Multistat III/Beckman	5	−3.6
Ektachem 400, 700/Kodak	39	−4.9
Electronuclear Gemini/ Electronucl	11	−5.6

[a]Calibration bias not significant, $p < .05$.

Source: J. W. Ross et al., "Matrix Effects and the Accuracy of Cholesterol Analysis," Archives of Pathology and Laboratory Medicine, 117:4 (1993), 393.

Veterans Affairs Laboratory Study

A study similar to the CAP and CDC investigation was undertaken in 112 VA laboratories in conjunction with CDC.[13] Because VA has the nation's largest hospital system, it provides insight into large-scale efforts to standardize cholesterol measurements. Briefly, the VA research group asked participating laboratories to conduct analyses of fresh serum samples and 1990 CAP quality control materials, permitting comparisons of how well instruments analyzed both types of specimens. This study team found "significant matrix-effect biases with the CAP Survey materials in six of the eight major peer [instrument] groups, despite the fact that accuracy of cholesterol measurements was maintained with fresh serum samples."[14] The authors concluded that "CAP PT [proficiency testing] materials used currently do not behave in a manner identical to fresh human serum when measuring cholesterol on many, but not all, analytic systems."[15] Table 3.2 presents the study findings.

[13]There are 174 VA Medical Center outpatient clinics and clinical laboratories that participate in the VA-CDC National Cholesterol Standardization and Certification Program. Of the laboratories in this program, 87 percent had an overall analytic bias of 5 percent or less from the reference method values, and 63.2 percent had an overall analytic bias of 3 percent or less.

[14]H. K. Naito et al., "Matrix Effects on Proficiency Testing Materials: Impact on Accuracy of Cholesterol Measurement in Laboratories in the Nation's Largest Hospital System," Archives of Pathology and Laboratory Medicine, 117:4 (1993), 345.

[15]Naito et al., p. 345.

Table 3.2: Matrix Effects for a Group of Instruments Used in VA Medical Center Laboratories

Instrument peer group	Number of laboratories	Bias average (+1 standard deviation in percent)	p[a]
DuPont Dimension	7	−8.9 ± 1.6	0.001
Beckman CX4, CX5, CX7	12	−5.5 ± 1.4	0.001
Kodak Ektachem	47	4.4 ± 2.2	0.001
Instrumentation Laboratory Monarch	5	−3.1 ± 0.8	0.002
Baxter Paramax	7	−2.4 ± 1.0	0.001
Technicon SMAC, RA	10	1.3 ± 1.7	0.05
Hitachi/BMD 707-747	10	0.4 ± 2.2	[b]
Abbott Spectrum, EPX	5	−0.3 ± 1.1	[b]

[a]Student's t test using 2-tailed test indicates the significance of matrix effect biases.

[b]Not significant at the 95-percent confidence level.

Source: H. K. Naito et al., "Matrix Effects on Proficiency Testing Materials: Impact on Accuracy of Cholesterol Measurement in Laboratories in the Nation's Largest Hospital System," Archives of Pathology and Laboratory Medicine, 117:4 (1993), 349.

The VA study authors noted that the biases that arise from matrix effects will cause incorrect conclusions about the accuracy of laboratory procedures done on fresh patient specimens. Further, matrix effects will "severely hamper interlaboratory accuracy transfer, standardization efforts, and monitoring performance of a laboratory's testing accuracy . . . ."[16]

Accuracy and Precision of Desk-Top Instruments

Cholesterol is often measured with small, portable and semiportable devices called desk-top analyzers, in either a physician's office or a nontraditional setting such as a health fair. Desk-top systems generally use the same kinds of enzymatic methods employed in laboratory settings.

NCEP guidelines do not differentiate between desk-top analyzers and those used in laboratories; all such devices are held to the same overall accuracy standards. A recent study that summarized desk-top analyzers concluded: "In general, desk-top analyzers give fairly accurate measurements on average, but tend to be somewhat more variable than laboratory-based

[16]Naito et al., p. 345.

methods in individual samples."[17] The same article links this difference in part to the use of fingerstick blood samples with these analyzers, the results of which are likely to differ from venous samples. Other factors that contribute to their measurement variability include lack of operator training and use of such devices in field settings where frequent transportation and changes in temperature and humidity can affect test results.

We identified 13 recent studies that evaluated desk-top analyzer performance. We discuss several of these studies in this section, focusing on those that permit comparison of data across devices. The first study evaluated five analyzers under tightly controlled conditions: Analyst (DuPont), Ektachem DT-60 (Eastman Kodak), Reflotron (Boehringer-Mannheim Diagnostics), Seralyzer (Ames Division, Miles Laboratories), and Vision (Abbott Laboratories). In terms of accuracy of total cholesterol measurements, the Ektachem DT-60 and the Vision had biases of less than 2.0 percent, within the current NCEP bias goal of <3 percent. The three other instruments had biases ranging from $\overline{5}.2$ percent to 10.4 percent, thus exceeding the NCEP goal (see table 3.3).

Table 3.3: Accuracy of Desk-Top Cholesterol Analyzers

Analyze	Value (mmol/L)	Analyst[a]	Kodak Ektachem	Reflotron	Seralyzer	Vision
Total cholesterol	5.17	9.7%	1.6%	6.3%	9.8%	1.3%
	6.21	10.4	1.4	5.2	9.7	0.8
HDL cholesterol	0.78	−12.7	6.0			29.7
	1.29	−10.4	6.0			8.2
LDL cholesterol	1.81	−9.6	6.3			−1.3
	3.36	18.7	2.2			0.8
	4.14	17.2	1.3			0.1
Triglyceride	1.13	6.0	−5.0			−10.0
	1.58	3.6	−3.6			−7.9
	2.03	1.7	−2.8			−6.1

[a]To convert mmol/L to mg/dL, multiply these values by 38.7. Thus, 5.17 mmol/L equals 200 mg/dL, and 6.21 mmol/L equals 240 mg/dL.

Source: H. W. Kaufman et al., "How Reliably Can Compact Chemistry Analyzers Measure Lipids?" Journal of the American Medical Association, 263:9 (1990), 1247.

[17]P. S. Bachorik and R. Rock, "Cholesterol Analysis with Desk-Top Analyzers," Methods for Clinical Laboratory Measurement of Lipid and Lipoprotein Risk Factors, N. Rifai and G. R. Warnick (eds.) (Washington, D.C.: AACC Press, 1991), p. 131.

Only three of the five analyzers tested could conduct HDL and LDL cholesterol analyses. Across the three HDL cholesterol levels tested, Kodak Ektachem DT-60 had results that were approximately 6.0-percent higher than the true value while the Analyst and Vision analyses of the low HDL cholesterol measure were –12.7 percent below and 29.7 percent above the true value, respectively. LDL cholesterol measures, derived with the Friedewald equation, conducted on the Kodak Ektachem DT-60 and Vision had an error of less than 3.0 percent while the Analyst exceeded 17 percent at both LDL cholesterol levels tested. The consequence of such error is that the correct total, HDL, and LDL cholesterol value is systematically over- or underestimated.

Data on the precision of these analyzers are presented in table 3.4. Note that the coefficient of variation of the Reflotron and Seralyzer for total cholesterol is 10 percent or higher, exceeding the current NCEP precision goal of ≤ 3 percent.

Table 3.4: Precision of Desk-Top Cholesterol Analyzers[a]

Analyze	Number of pairs	Analyst	Kodak Ektachem	Reflotron	Seralyzer	Vision
Total cholesterol	96					
Mean		6.28	5.79	6.03	6.26	5.77
SD		0.16	0.15	0.80	0.63	0.11
CV%		2.6	2.5	13.3	10.2	2.0
HDL cholesterol	39					
Mean		1.09	1.27			1.34
SD		0.07	0.03			0.12
CV%		6.4	2.5			9.0
LDL cholesterol	39					
Mean		5.25	4.53			4.47
SD		0.21	0.11			0.19
CV%		4.0	2.5			4.3
Triglyceride	39					
Mean		1.59	1.4			1.42
SD		0.08	0.03			0.08
CV%		5.3	2.0			5.2

[a]Neither group has set LDL accuracy standards. Standard deviation (SD) is derived by taking the square root of the variance. With a normal distribution, 68 percent of the values are encompassed by +1 standard deviation, 95 percent by +2 standard deviations, and 99.7 percent by +3 standard deviations. Coefficient of variation (CV) expresses the standard deviation as a percentage of the mean value and is used in clinical chemistry to compare precision at different concentration levels. A method's precision varies inversely with the coefficient of variation: the lower it is, the more precise the method.

Source: H. W. Kaufman et al., "How Reliably Can Compact Chemistry Analyzers Measure Lipids?" Journal of the American Medical Association, 263:9 (1990), 1247.

Another perspective on the data in the preceding tables is how the results could influence the risk category into which a patient is classified (desirable, borderline-high risk, or high risk for coronary heart disease). Two instruments, the Kodak Ektachem DT-60 and Abbott Vision, correctly classified 95 percent and 94 percent of the total cholesterol specimens, respectively. The Analyst, Reflotron, and Seralyzer correctly classified 74 percent, 83 percent, and 75 percent of patient total cholesterol specimens, respectively.

A second study we reviewed that was published in 1993 also evaluated five desk-top devices used to measure cholesterol in screening environments, assessing bias, precision, and patient misclassification error for capillary and venous whole blood and venous plasma. The devices were the Ektachem DT-60 (Kodak), Liposcan (Home Diagnostics), QuickRead (Photest), Reflotron (Boehringer-Mannheim), and Vision (Abbott).[18] The authors concluded that none of these devices met the NCEP performance recommendations regarding bias and precision. Of interest were findings regarding average percentage bias, which differed for capillary and venous whole blood (see table 3.5) and misclassification rates (see table 3.6), which ranged from false negative rates as high as 37 to 48 percent for the Liposcan to false positives up to 38 and 34 percent for the QuickRead. Misclassification into false positive categories was 18 percent for the Vision, 14 percent for the Reflotron, and 7 percent for the Ektachem DT-60.

Table 3.5: Average Percentage Bias for Cholesterol for Four Desk-Top Devices

Device	Capillary blood	Venous blood	Venous plasma
Reflotron	4.1%	−0.8%	−0.3%
Vision	8.4	4.0	3.6
Kodak DT-60	2.6	a	2.4
QuickRead	18.4	16.5	1.8

[a]Not available.

Source: W. G. Miller et al., "Total Error Assessment of Five Methods for Cholesterol Screening," Clinical Chemistry, 39:2 (1993), 299.

Table 3.6: Test Results Misclassified for Five Desk-Top Devices[a]

Device	Capillary blood		Venous blood		Venous plasma	
	False negative	False positive	False negative	False positive	False negative	False positive
Reflotron	2.2%	14.1%	7.1%	3.1%	2.1%	4.1%
Vision	0	18.3	0	5.7	0	5.7
DT-60	4.4	6.7	b	b	2.0	5.1
QuickRead	0	37.5	0	34.0	1.6	11.5
Liposcan	36.8	2.6	47.5	0	b	b

[a]False negative refers to a test result reported to the patient that is incorrectly low. A patient in this situation may not be treated but should be considered, according to NCEP guidelines. False positive refers to a test result reported to the patient that is incorrectly high. In this situation, a person may be treated when that is unnecessary, according to NCEP guidelines.

[b]Not available.

Source: W. G. Miller et al., "Total Error Assessment of Five Methods for Cholesterol Screening," Clinical Chemistry, 39:2 (1993), 300.

[18]W. G. Miller et al., "Total Error Assessment of Five Methods for Cholesterol Screening," Clinical Chemistry, 39:2 (1993), 297-304.

Home Test Devices

Home test kits to measure total cholesterol have also been cleared by FDA and have recently begun to be marketed directly to consumers (they have been available to physicians since 1991). Total cholesterol results obtained with the AccuMeter, currently the only such device being marketed in the United States, for 100 patients were compared with a CDC-standardized laboratory at the Medical College of Virginia.[19] While AccuMeter's results met NCEP guidelines for measurement bias (<3 percent) for both capillary and venous blood when using a mean bias measure, these researchers found that mean absolute percentage bias was 5.7 percent and 5.2 percent, respectively.[20] In addition, 18 to 20 percent of samples fell outside the +8.9 percent of the reference result, the level the NCEP established for acceptable total error for single cholesterol measurements. Figures for precision, from 40 total cholesterol assays done in duplicate from three pools of human serum with mean concentrations of 182 mg/dL, 223 mg/dL, and 266 mg/dL, exceeded NCEP/LSP guidelines (<3 percent precision error); the coefficients of variation were 4.5 percent, 5.4 percent, and 5.8 percent, respectively. The authors noted that approximately 5 percent of the devices did not function properly and could not provide a cholesterol reading.

We met with FDA officials to discuss their decision to permit marketing of the AccuMeter under 510(k) regulations. They explained that it met the criteria of "substantial equivalence" to an analyzer currently being marketed, therefore complying with existing regulations, although the device does not meet NCEP standards for precision and accuracy (as judged by "traceability" to the Abell-Kendall reference method).

---

[19]J. McKenney and W. G. Miller, "A Perspective on Home Cholesterol Testing," The Fats of Life, 7:4 (1993), 1-7.

[20]The mean bias measure reflects the average difference from the reference value, taking into consideration negative and positive differences; the mean absolute bias measure does not take into account negative and positive differences and reflects the average of the absolute difference from the reference value.

Chapter 4

Factors That Influence the Variability of Cholesterol Levels

Even if a single cholesterol measurement were analytically accurate and precise, it would not reflect how a person's cholesterol can vary from day to day. Total, HDL, and LDL cholesterol levels vary over time and are influenced by what are termed preanalytic or biological factors that include behavioral (exercise, diet, alcohol consumption), clinical (disease, pregnancy), and sample collection conditions. In this chapter, we answer our third evaluation question: What factors influence cholesterol levels?

Scientific literature indicates that some variation and fluctuation of an individual's total, HDL, and LDL cholesterol is normal and to be expected. For instance, in some individuals, week-to-week fluctuations can be dramatic while in others virtually no change may occur over the same time period. Overall, biological variation of total cholesterol is reported to average 6.1 percent; HDL cholesterol variation averages 7.4 percent; LDL biological variability, 9.5 percent; triglycerides, 22.6 percent. These findings suggest that variation in cholesterol levels is normal and, for some individuals, can be quite pronounced. The implication for testing, particularly for patients near a cutpoint (such as 240 mg/dL) is that repeated measurements may be necessary. In light of measurement uncertainty for HDL and LDL, multiple measures of these subfractions may be warranted, particularly before making a diagnosis.

Other factors—diet, exercise, alcohol intake—appear to have differing effects on individuals' cholesterol levels. The amount of the effect varies depending on the amount and duration of intake and physiological factors. In some, it may not have a large effect on total and LDL cholesterol levels. This may be partially related to the estimates that one third of an individual's cholesterol level is linked to diet while the body produces the remaining two thirds. The evidence regarding regular exercise points to the benefits associated with such activity, as measured by changes in lipid levels. While alcohol intake can have a positive effect on cholesterol levels, consumption must be balanced with the potential risks associated with it. The potential effect of diet on cholesterol levels was noted in the 1990 NCEP report on cholesterol measurement, which recommended that patients maintain their usual diet and that their weight be stable for at least 2 weeks before their cholesterol level is measured.

Clinical factors such as disease, pregnancy, and some medications (diuretics, beta blockers, oral contraceptives) can also alter cholesterol levels. How a blood specimen is taken can also have a crucial role in cholesterol analysis. Some research has found that fingerstick (capillary) samples differed markedly from venous samples when analyzed by the same device while other researchers have called for more standardized specimen collection techniques.

Biological Variation

Cholesterol levels within a person vary over time, depending on a number of factors. As discussed in chapter 1, for example, as people age, their total cholesterol level tends to increase. However, cholesterol levels can also vary considerably between measurements because of what is termed intra-individual biological variability—that is, normal fluctuations in cholesterol levels are estimated to account for about 65 percent of the total intra-individual variation for both total and HDL cholesterol and about 95 percent of the variation for triglycerides. Studies have linked other types of biological variation to diet, alcohol intake, smoking, and physical activity. The body of literature on this subject is large: a 1992 article reviewed more than 300 publications, most of which had been published within the previous 5 years.[1]

A recent statistical synthesis of findings from 30 studies published between 1970 and 1992 provides considerable information on intra-individual biological variation—that is, the normal fluctuation in cholesterol levels referred to above. According to this review, total cholesterol is the most stable lipid, with the day-to-day biological variation averaging 6.1 percent; variations in HDL cholesterol concentrations, 7.4 percent; LDL biological variability, 9.5 percent; triglyceride, 22.6 percent.[2]

The number of subjects in the selected studies of total cholesterol variability ranged from small (less than 20) to quite large (14,600). Not surprisingly, the number of specimens and the sampling intervals varied as well. Two large studies analyzed two specimens, taken 1 month apart, while another study with a smaller number of subjects analyzed specimens taken twice a week for 10 weeks. Results for HDL variability were based on 16 studies, triglyceride variability 19 studies, and LDL variation 10 studies.

Two recent articles have also reported similar findings. One study compared total cholesterol and HDL measurements taken from 40 male subjects 1 week apart. The authors found a relatively wide range of

[1]G. R. Cooper et al., "Blood Lipid Measurements: Variations and Practical Utility," Journal of the American Medical Association, 267:12 (1992), 1652-59.

[2]S. J. Smith et al., "Biological Variability in Concentrations of Serum Lipids: Sources of Variation among Results from Published Studies and Composite Predicted Values," Clinical Chemistry, 39:6 (1993), 1012-22.

variability in some patients: one patient's total cholesterol declined dramatically from one week to the next, dropping from nearly 300 mg/dL to just over 220 mg/dL, while several others' total cholesterol level scarcely moved between the two tests (the coefficient of variation for single measurements was 6.8 percent for total cholesterol and 10.5 percent for HDL, slightly higher than the figures from the statistical synthesis reported earlier).[3]

Another study of cholesterol variability tracked 20 subjects 22 to 63 years old measuring their total, LDL, and HDL cholesterol weekly for 4 weeks. The authors found variations of more than +20 percent in the serum levels of total cholesterol, LDL, and HDL in 75 percent, 95 percent, and 65 percent of the subjects, respectively. More important, 40 percent moved in or out of one of the risk categories, and 10 percent moved two categories—from "desirable" to "high risk."[4]

Other research has found that LDL and total cholesterol levels within individuals vary by season, both averaging 2.5-percent higher in the winter than the summer. The HDL cholesterol level, however, has not been found to vary seasonally. Women are affected by another aspect of biological variability; total cholesterol concentrations may average 20 percent lower during the luteal phase (the period immediately after ovulation) of the menstrual cycle.

Behavioral Factors

Cholesterol levels vary because of behavioral factors, and some of this variability can influence short-term measurements. For example, strenuous exercise 24 hours prior to having a blood specimen taken can elevate an individual's HDL cholesterol level. Likewise, moderate alcohol consumption can increase HDL and decrease LDL cholesterol levels. Behavior over longer periods of time can also affect cholesterol levels—diet, alcohol consumption, exercise. The relevance to the measurement theme of this report is that there is more to variation in cholesterol levels than inaccurate laboratory tests.

Diet and Cholesterol

Consumption of certain saturated fatty acids and, to a lesser extent, cholesterol is linked to higher serum LDL cholesterol values. In terms of

[3]R. H. Christenson et al., "Improving the Reliability of Total and High-Density Lipoprotein Cholesterol Measurements," Archives of Pathology and Laboratory Medicine, 115 (1991), 1212-16.

[4]M. Mogadam et al., "Within-Person Fluctuations of Serum Cholesterol and Lipoproteins," Archives of Internal Medicine, 150 (1990), 1645-48.

diet, an increase in cholesterol intake of about 100 mg (per 4,200 joules) raises plasma cholesterol by about 10 mg/dL. Progressively higher cholesterol intakes exceeding 500 mg appear to have smaller incremental effects on cholesterol levels.[5] The same study points out that dietary cholesterol is incompletely and variably absorbed by individuals, ranging from 18 to 75 percent. Further, people with the highest LDL cholesterol levels appear to have the highest percentage of absorption of dietary cholesterol.

How individuals respond to different diets varies, however. One recent synthesis of literature on diet and health points out that

"blood cholesterol responses of individuals differ substantially in response to changes in dietary lipids . . . . For the same increase in dietary cholesterol or saturated fat, the cholesterol levels of most persons will increase, but some will remain essentially unchanged and a few will increase dramatically."[6]

As noted in chapter 2, only one third of an individual's cholesterol is derived from diet and the remaining two thirds are manufactured by the liver.

In terms of the contribution that diet can make to cholesterol reduction, the 1993 NCEP guidelines state that men who follow the step I diet could expect their total cholesterol level to be reduced 5 to 7 percent while those who follow the more restrictive step II could expect an 8-to-14 percent reduction. These estimates are based on models derived from metabolic ward studies (done on institutionalized patients), which closely monitored and controlled individuals' adherence to their diet. Some researchers have noted that such reductions can be difficult to achieve in a "free living" population.

Alcohol Intake

Published epidemiological studies have demonstrated a relationship between alcohol intake and changes in cholesterol profiles. The amount of change attributed to alcohol depends on the amount consumed, individual susceptibility, genetic variables, and diet. Moderate alcohol intake (defined as several drinks a day) appears to increase HDL cholesterol and may be associated with reduced risk of coronary heart disease. Greater alcohol consumption is also associated with a lowering of LDL cholesterol and an increase in triglycerides. In one study, it is estimated that 4 to

[5]G. R. Cooper et al., p. 1653.

[6]Walter Willett, Nutritional Epidemiology (New York: Oxford University Press, 1990), p. 362.

6 percent of the variance of HDL cholesterol levels in the population may be linked to alcohol consumption.

Exercise

Exercise has been shown to influence cholesterol levels and has received increased attention as having a preventive effect on coronary heart disease. Researchers have found that exercise that is strenuous and promotes endurance causes LDL, triglycerides, and apo B to decrease while raising HDL and apo AI levels. Other evidence regarding exercise points to the benefits of brisk walking. One study found that previously sedentary women who walked an average of 155 minutes per week decreased their total cholesterol level by 6.5 percent compared with a decrease of 2.2 percent in control subjects, and the HDL level of walkers increased 27 percent, compared with a 2-percent increase in controls.[7] A recent article suggests that the effect of these changes depends on the volume, intensity, and type of exercise undertaken, a slight variation on earlier work.[8]

Apart from longer-term effects, acute exercise also causes a significant rise in HDL levels such that it is recommended that patients avoid any strenuous exercise 24 hours prior to having a blood specimen taken.[9]

Obesity

Obese individuals have been found to have higher total and LDL cholesterol and triglyceride levels and lower HDL cholesterol when compared to nonobese members of control groups. When an obese individual loses weight, a decline in triglyceride level occurs (about 40 percent); total and LDL cholesterol levels are found to decline about 10 percent while the HDL level increases about 10 percent. The implication for cholesterol measurements, particularly for obese individuals who repeatedly gain and lose weight, is that such fluctuations can be the source of significant variation in lipoprotein levels.[10] In fact, NCEP/LSP recommended that an

---

[7]A. E. Hardman et al., "Brisk Walking and Plasma High-Density Lipoprotein Cholesterol Concentration in Previously Sedentary Women," British Medical Journal, 299 (1989), 1204-9.

[8]P. A. Taylor and A. Ward, "Women, High-Density Lipoprotein Cholesterol, and Exercise," Archives of Internal Medicine, 153 (1993), 1178-84.

[9]N. Rifai et al., "Preanalytical Variations in Lipid, Lipoprotein, and Apolipoprotein Testing," in Methods for Clinical Laboratory Measurement of Lipid and Lipoprotein Risk Factors, N. Rifai and G. R. Warnick (eds.) (Washington, D.C.: AACC Press, 1991), p. 23.

[10]Cooper et al., p. 1653.

individual's weight be stable and that he or she maintain his or her usual diet for at least 2 weeks prior to having cholesterol measured.[11]

Clinical Factors

A person's cholesterol profile can be affected by acute, infectious, and metabolic diseases, and some types of medications have been linked with elevated levels in some patient groups.

Disease

Several conditions are associated with increased cholesterol levels. Diabetes mellitus and hypothyroidism are cited as the most common of these, with total cholesterol and LDL cholesterol levels being elevated in 30 percent of the patients with the latter condition. Patients with diabetes mellitus sometimes have elevated triglycerides, and higher levels of insulin are positively associated with unfavorable levels of total and LDL cholesterol, triglycerides, apo B, and blood pressure, and negatively with HDL cholesterol components.

Acute myocardial infarction is associated with decreases in levels of total cholesterol, LDL, apo AI, and apo B. Indeed, lipid levels after a heart attack are affected to such a degree that it is recommended that blood specimens be obtained within 24 hours of the event; if they cannot be taken within 24 hours, then they should not be taken for 3 months because the test will not accurately reflect the patient's usual lipid level. Other diseases such as Tay-Sachs, rheumatoid arthritis, and infections can also alter lipid profiles.[12] In addition, familial hypercholesterolemia and other related disorders are associated with increased blood cholesterol levels.

Drug-Induced Variations and Pregnancy

Medication can also alter lipid levels. Diuretics, some beta blockers, and sex steroids have been cited as changing lipid levels. Oral contraceptives high in progestin can increase serum total and LDL cholesterol and decrease HDL cholesterol levels, while contraceptives with high estrogen content can cause opposite changes. Similar changes have been found in postmenopausal women taking estrogen supplements.[13]

Pregnancy is associated with changes in lipid profiles in the second and third trimesters, when total and LDL cholesterol, triglyceride, apo AI, apo

---

[11]National Cholesterol Education Program, Recommendations for Improving Cholesterol Measurement (Bethesda, Md.: 1990).

[12]Rifai et al., p. 23.

[13]Rifai et al., p. 24.

AII, and apo B are significantly increased. Because of these changes, lipid levels are affected to the degree that testing is not recommended until 3 months postpartum or 3 months following cessation of lactation.

Laboratory Factors

How a blood specimen is collected and handled may affect lipid levels. For example, blood cholesterol samples are often drawn when the patient is in a fasting state, particularly when a lipid profile is to be taken. This is because eating a typical fat-containing meal causes a patient's lipid profile to change, an effect that lasts about 9 hours. Typically, triglyceride levels increase as does very-low-density lipoprotein (VLDL), while LDL cholesterol falls significantly.

The source of the blood specimen taken can also influence measured cholesterol levels. Here the issue of concern is whether the sample source is capillary (taken from a finger) or venous (taken from a vein). One large research study found that capillary blood total cholesterol was approximately 7-percent higher than venous blood samples when both were analyzed with the same analyzer. According to this same study,

"the most reliable screening measurements were obtained when the analyses were performed in venous plasma samples by a qualified clinical laboratory. . . . The most-variable measurements were obtained with the capillary samples, and these measurements seemed to be most prone to misclassification overall."[14]

A 1993 article briefly discusses the difference between venous and capillary samples, pointing out "contradictory results" (that is, some studies reporting either higher or lower capillary results than venous results, depending on the various procedures and devices tested) and a lack of consensus in the literature about such differences. The study's authors conclude that "capillary collection technique is critical and must be standardized to obtain reliable cholesterol results."[15]

How the specimen is taken and prepared for analysis also can affect lipid level measurements. Here factors such as the knowledge and experience of the laboratory technician are important. For example, the length of time a person is sitting or standing prior to having the specimen taken has been demonstrated to influence cholesterol test results. Patients should remain

---

[14]P. S. Bachorik et al., "Cholesterol Screening: Comparative Evaluation of On-Site and Laboratory-Based Measurements," Clinical Chemistry, 36:2 (1990), 259.

[15]G. W. Miller et al., "Total Error Assessment of Five Methods for Cholesterol Screening," Clinical Chemistry, 39:2 (1993), 302.

seated for at least 15 minutes before a venous sample is taken, and if a tourniquet is used, it should be applied for less than 1 minute before the specimen used for a lipid analysis is taken.[16] Proper storage of samples is also important to avoid changes in the composition of samples and to ensure accurate measurement results. Use of a standard collection policy by trained laboratory technicians can help minimize variability associated with these factors.

[16]Rifai et al., p. 27.

Chapter 5

The Potential Effect of Measurement Uncertainty and Agency Comments and Our Response

In this chapter, we discuss the study's fourth evaluation question: What is the potential effect of uncertain measurement? This is followed by our conclusions and discussion of agency comments.

Addressing Measurement Error

Progress has been made in improving analytical accuracy in cholesterol measurement, with the development of better methods and materials in recent years. Yet, despite the attention cholesterol has received, it continues to be difficult to measure with accuracy and consistency across the broad range of devices and settings in which it is analyzed. While several studies have found that accuracy with patient samples was good, problems with matrix effects from using processed quality control materials have occurred, thus making it difficult to adequately assess accuracy among laboratories. In addition, the lack of information on accuracy in many laboratory settings where patients are likely to be tested, such as commercial laboratories, physicians' offices, and mass screening locations, makes it impossible to know whether the accuracy goals established for total and HDL cholesterol are uniformly being met.

Even if one could be certain that a laboratory could provide reasonably accurate and precise test results, biological and behavioral factors such as diet, excercise, or illness cause an individual's cholesterol level to vary. It has been estimated that such factors may account for up to 65 percent of the total variation in an individual's reported cholesterol measurement. Studies have documented that some individuals' cholesterol level can vary dramatically from week to week while others' remains relatively constant. Although some biological variation can be controlled for, by having patients maintain their weight and diet for a modest period prior to measurement, many factors cannot be controlled.

Total error from both analytical and biological variability can be considerable, as shown in tables 5.1 and 5.2, where calculations are made for hypothetical total and HDL cholesterol test results at different specified levels. For the purposes of this analysis, which is intended to illustrate the potential range of variability around an actual or known cholesterol level, we used the current goals for total analytical error (+8.9 percent for total cholesterol according to NCEP and +30 percent for HDL according to HCFA) and what is currently known about biological variability from a synthesis of studies (6.1 percent for total cholesterol and 7.4 percent for HDL cholesterol). Both analytical and biological variability can of course be lower or higher than these figures, depending on a combination of factors.

Table 5.1: The Effect of Analytical and Biological Variability on Total Cholesterol Test Results[a]

	Potential range		
Test result	Based on analytical variability alone[b]	Based on biological variability alone[c]	Based on total variability[d]
180	164-196	158-202	151-209
200	182-218	176-224	167-233
220	200-240	193-247	184-256
240	219-261	211-269	201-279
260	237-283	228-292	218-302

[a]Values are mg/dL.

[b]Calculated using the NCEP Laboratory Standardization Panel goal of ±8.9 percent (0.05 level, 2-tailed test). The total analytic error of 8.9 percent is derived by summing the precision and bias components in the following manner:

$$3 + 1.96 \sqrt{3^2}.$$

[c]Calculated using an estimate of intraindividual biological variability (6.1 percent coefficient of variation) derived from a meta-analysis of 30 studies by S. J. Smith et al., "Biological Variability in Concentrations of Serum Lipids: Sources of Variation Among Results from Published Studies and Composite Predicted Values," Clinical Chemistry, 39:6 (1993).

[d]Total percentage error calculated from the following expression:

$$3 + 1.96 \sqrt{3^2 + 6.1^2}.$$

Table 5.2: The Effect of Analytical and Biological Variability on HDL Cholesterol Test Results[a]

	Potential range		
Test result	Based on analytical variability alone[b]	Based on biological variability alone[c]	Based on total variability[d]
15	11-20	13-17	10-20
25	18-33	21-29	17-33
35	25-46	30-40	24-46
45	32-59	38-52	31-59
55	39-72	47-63	38-72

[a]Values are mg/dL.

[b]Calculated using the HCFA goal of ±30 percent.

[c]Calculated using an estimate of intraindividual biological variability (7.4 percent coefficient of variation) derived from a meta-analysis of 16 studies by S. J. Smith et al., "Biological Variability in Concentrations of Serum Lipids: Sources of Variation among Results from Published Studies and Composite Predicted Values," Clinical Chemistry, 39.6 (1993).

[d]Calculated as the square root of the sum of analytical variability squared plus biological variability squared (30.9 percent).

The results in tables 5.1 and 5.2 show that a single cholesterol measurement may be highly misleading with respect to an individual's actual cholesterol value. A total cholesterol value that is known to be 240 mg/dL, for example, may vary as much as 16 percent or range from 201 to 279 mg/dL, when using these error rate assumptions. Similar estimates for HDL cholesterol measurements are presented in table 5.2.

The implication of these estimates is that cholesterol levels should be thought of in terms of ranges rather than absolute fixed numbers. Compensating for variation by using the average of at least two cholesterol measurements is in line with the current NCEP guidelines and recent literature on the subject.[1] The most recent NCEP Adult Treatment Panel recommends that a second test be done when an initial measurement has found that total cholesterol exceeds 200 mg/dL and HDL is under 35 mg/dL. In terms of HDL and LDL cholesterol, which have been documented to have analytical and biological variation somewhat higher than total cholesterol, more variability can be expected. CDC officials we interviewed emphasized that considerable scientific work remains before HDL measurement is as well understood as total cholesterol. Authors of a recent study in Clinical Chemistry therefore recommend that as many as four HDL and LDL cholesterol tests be done before making treatment decisions.[2]

A practical way to address the problem of measurement variability is to compare multiple tests using a technique termed "relative range."[3] Relative range is calculated by dividing the range—the difference between two values—by the mean. For example, if a patient has two total cholesterol results of 240 and 200 mg/dL, you would divide 40 by 220 to determine the relative range, which is 0.18. The relative range, according to the researchers who developed this method, should be less than or equal to 0.16 for two specimens. For the example just given, a third test would be needed, and the goal would be to achieve a relative range of less than or

---

[1]The effect of a second test on the range of variability around a known cholesterol level can be illustrated with our previous hypothetical example, in which analytical and biological variability are combined. For a total cholesterol value of 240 mg/dL, the total percentage error would be about 12 percent when factoring in a second measurement, thus narrowing the variability to a range of 210 to 270 mg/dL.

[2]S. J. Smith et al., "Biological Variability in Concentrations of Serum Lipids: Sources of Variation among Results from Published Studies and Composite Predicted Values," Clinical Chemistry, 39:6 (1993), 1021.

[3]G. R. Cooper et al., "Estimating and Minimizing Effects of Biologic Sources of Variation by Relative Range when Measuring the Mean of Serum Lipids and Lipoproteins," Clinical Chemistry, 40:2 (1994), 227-32.

equal to 0.19; with four specimens, the relative range should be less than or equal to 0.21.[4]

Implications of Measurement Variability

Having accurate and precise cholesterol measurements is important, given the central role that cholesterol measurement has in classifying, evaluating, and treating patients deemed at risk of coronary heart disease. As noted in chapter 1, the average total cholesterol level for U.S. adults 20 years old and older is about 205 mg/dL, which puts them within the NCEP-defined borderline-high risk category. Moreover, 29 percent of U.S. adults, 52 million people, have a cholesterol level that is classified as too high, making them candidates for dietary therapy. Of this group, an estimated 12.7 million adults, one third of whom have established coronary heart disease, might be considered candidates for drug therapy to lower their cholesterol level. Once drug therapy is initiated, it may need to be maintained for life.

Although the NCEP guidelines recognize the problem of measurement variability and the guidelines stress the need for multiple measurements, important consequences can be associated with measurement error. The potential exists, for example, that physicians may not account for measurement problems and may base decisions about patients on incorrect test results. In a worst-case scenario, two types of diagnostic errors could occur: false-positive or false-negative screens. A false-positive screen could result in treating individuals who in fact have a desirable total, HDL, and LDL cholesterol level. A false-negative result would incorrectly reassure an individual that his or her cholesterol level is low. The risk of misclassification would be greatest for those whose measured cholesterol levels are closest to one of the cutpoints. There is less ambiguity when values are well above or below a cutpoint. The likelihood of such errors occurring, however, is greater if physicians rely on only a single cholesterol measurement in making treatment decisions.

Continuing efforts are needed to improve the accuracy and precision of lipid measurements so that medical decisions to initiate and continue treatment to lower elevated cholesterol levels can be both effective and efficient. To minimize misclassification problems, it is also important to ensure that physicians who evaluate and treat patients with elevated cholesterol levels are knowledgeable about measurement variability and the need to conduct multiple tests.

---

[4]For further information on relative range, see G. R. Cooper et al., "Blood Lipid Measurements: Variations and Practical Utility," Journal of the American Medical Association, 267:12 (1992), 1652-59.

Agency Comments and Our Response

Officials from HHS reviewed a draft of this report and provided written comments, reproduced in appendix I. In addition, HHS provided draft technical comments that we have incorporated in the text where appropriate.

Overall, HHS officials believed that cholesterol measurement has improved substantially in recent years and that accuracy in laboratories across the country is better than what is presented in our report. Regarding general comments on the need for better standardization materials (lyophilized serum pools without matrix effects), we agree that this is a major challenge that must be addressed if measurement is to be improved. This point was made in NCEP's 1990 report on cholesterol measurement, indicating that this is not a new problem but rather one that was noted previously.

HHS did not concur with a recommendation we included in the draft report concerning an assessment of whether problems of patient "misclassification" result from measurement variability. It indicated that information on misclassification already exists and that additional work would only provide further definition of the issue rather than solving known problems such as the effect of matrix effects on measurement accuracy. We recognize that some information on this issue does exist and also understand that further efforts are currently under way, particularly by NIH and CDC, to assess how the NCEP guidelines are being implemented in practice and to evaluate overall laboratory performance. We have deleted our draft recommendation from the final report because these ongoing agency efforts should respond to our concerns about misclassification. We encourage HHS to continue this work and provide the results to the Congress and the general public.

The agency also suggested that the discussion of diet and clinical trials that we included in the draft was too brief. We have deleted this discussion from the final report and will address it in more depth in a later report we are preparing on the clinical trial base of information that supports the NCEP guidelines.

DEPARTMENT OF HEALTH & HUMAN SERVICES   Office of Inspector General

Washington, D.C. 20201

JUL 25 1994

Mr. Kwai-Cheung Chan
Director of Program Evaluation in
  Physical Systems Areas
United States General
  Accounting Office
Washington, D.C. 20548

Dear Mr. Chan:

Enclosed are the Department's comments on your draft report,
"Cholesterol Measurement: Test Accuracy and Factors that
Influence Cholesterol Levels." The comments represent the
tentative position of the Department and are subject to
reevaluation when the final version of this report is received.

The Department appreciates the opportunity to comment on this
draft report before its publication.

Sincerely yours,

June Gibbs Brown
Inspector General

Enclosure

COMMENTS OF THE DEPARTMENT OF HEALTH AND HUMAN SERVICES
ON THE GENERAL ACCOUNTING OFFICE (GAO) DRAFT REPORT
"CHOLESTEROL MEASUREMENT: TEST ACCURACY AND
FACTORS THAT INFLUENCE CHOLESTEROL LEVELS"

General Comments

The GAO draft report correctly identifies the problem of
matrix effects to be an important factor in the accuracy
problem of cholesterol testing. The draft report's proposed
recommendation calls for assessing in greater detail how much
misclassification of patients into risk categories is now
occurring, rather than a solution.

We believe the usefulness of the report would be increased if
GAO would describe the resources that will be needed to
resolve the problems identified. Standardization resources,
such as lyophilized serum pools without matrix effects for
total cholesterol, low-density lipoprotein (LDL) cholesterol
(bad cholesterol), high-density lipoprotein (HDL) cholesterol
(good cholesterol) and triglycerides, will have to be
developed to assure accurate measurements in clinical
laboratories. The reference methods used by the Centers for
Disease Control and Prevention (CDC) for HDL cholesterol, LDL
cholesterol, and triglycerides need to be documented and
checked for transferability in order for them to become
acceptable as national and international reference methods.
The CDC-used reference method for LDL cholesterol can attain a
CV (precision) of 1.2 percent, for HDL cholesterol a CV of
2.2 percent, for very-LDL cholesterol a CV of 12 percent and
for triglycerides a CV of 3 percent. These values are highly
acceptable for a reference method, but still must be
documented for acceptance by the USA-National Committee for
Clinical Laboratory Standards and the World Health
Organization. Clinical laboratories will have difficulty in
fully meeting the requirements of standardization and
proficiency testing programs, and the Health Care Financing
Administration evaluation of the Clinical Laboratory
Improvement Amendments' requirements for cholesterol and
related lipoprotein measurements will be impeded, until a
lyophilized serum free of matrix effects becomes available to
evaluate and monitor cholesterol measurements in clinical
laboratories.

A second problematic element of the draft report is that it
generally presents the negative aspects of the areas of diet
and clinical trials while neglecting much positive
information. We believe the draft report's discussions on
diet and clinical trials could be deleted from this report and
a balanced presentation included in the GAO's upcoming report
on the cholesterol science base. We believe the draft
report's discussion on diet and coronary heart disease (CHD)

2

does not cover this subject adequately, presents a skeptical
view of diet's potential to lower blood cholesterol that does
not fully reflect the existing science base, and is not
directly germane to a report on measurement accuracy. The
draft report cites several concerns that have been raised in
clinical trials without addressing the many positive aspects
of the trials. The areas of agreement as to who should
receive treatment far outweigh the areas of debate. We
believe that the report does not give an adequate picture of
the current state of scientific knowledge and consensus, and
in any case a discussion of the benefits and potential
consequences of cholesterol-lowering treatment is not directly
relevant to this report. In addition, drug treatment is
characterized as a life-long proposition that can be both
costly and unpleasant, without acknowledging that, when
warranted, drug therapy significantly reduces the risk of
illness and death from CHD.

We believe that the draft report should give adequate
attention to the performance of laboratories on fresh samples,
which is much better than on the test materials that are
subject to matrix effects. This point should be made early in
the report to provide a true picture of laboratory
performance. Data from a CDC-College of American Pathologists
collaboration are similarly used to draw negative findings,
but the good news in the paper about laboratory performance is
not given sufficient attention. In addition, we believe the
literature search should not have been restricted to the
period since 1988. Publication of the first report of the
National Cholesterol Education Program (NCEP) Laboratory
Standardization Panel in that year does not appear to provide
an adequate rationale for this choice. The role of the Food
and Drug Administration (FDA) and its mandate to clear safe
and effective in vitro diagnostic devices through the process
required by section 510(k) of the Food, Drug, and Cosmetic Act
is misunderstood, and FDA's efforts to ensure the accuracy of
cholesterol measuring devices is reduced to the clearance of a
single device, the AccuMeter. The prominent and long-standing
role of the National Heart, Lung, and Blood Institute and the
Lipid Research Clinics Program in fostering standardization is
not presented, nor is the joint effort of the National
Institutes of Health, CDC, and FDA recognized.

Finally, the impact of misclassification is discussed in an
abbreviated fashion and may be overstated. The association
between cholesterol and CHD is continuous so that the risk is
not subject to greater change at category boundaries
(cutpoints) than at other points on the curve. Thus, the
values near the cutpoints should be regarded with clinical
judgment, since there is not a great difference in CHD risk

3

between an LDL cholesterol of, for example, 155 milligrams per deciliter of blood (mg/dL) and an LDL cholesterol of 165 mg/dL. Moreover, the risk of CHD is multifactorial, and the NCEP Adult Treatment Panel II guidelines establish a hierarchy of risk categories which incorporates other CHD risk factors. Repeat determinations are recommended and will be done for many individuals and this will reduce the false positives. The repeat determination every 5 years for those who have had only one determination gives a measure of protection to the false negatives. These considerations would tend to reduce the impact of misclassification. We believe the draft report relies too heavily on estimates of misclassification derived from a single specimen. Physicians will use two specimens most of the time for evaluation of the serial cholesterol values of a patient. The draft report needs to indicate tolerance limits for all total and lipoprotein cholesterol determinations from serial measurements (See Clinical Chemistry 1994;40:227).

GAO Recommendation

The Secretary of HHS should examine the following issue that affects cholesterol testing.

In light of (1) the importance placed on cholesterol levels as CHD risk indicators, (2) the number of people currently considered to need, or who may be undergoing, drug or dietary therapy, and (3) the potential error associated with cholesterol testing, it is important to know the extent to which misclassification of patients occurs. HHS should devise a strategy to collect and analyze information on this issue. The collaborative studies between CDC and other groups mentioned in this report provide evidence such studies are possible. Expanding work beyond these settings to a sample of physician office laboratories and screening settings that predominate in the testing arena--and where less accurate and precise desk-top analyzers are more likely to be used--should be undertaken to determine whether or not patients are being given correct test results and being misclassified into risk categories.

HHS Comments

We do not concur with this recommendation. As noted in our general comments, the recommended actions would not remedy the matrix problem that this report identifies as an important factor in the problem of accuracy in cholesterol measurement. A body of information on misclassification already exists and it is unlikely the additional details that would be obtained from implementing this recommendation would reveal much more of import. As noted in the report, characterizing the

4

universe of sites at which cholesterol testing is performed is
difficult. To better assess how much misclassification occurs
at the various sites would require substantial resources.
Yet, such an effort would yield only a further definition of
the problem.

It is the view of the Department that it would be more
appropriate to devote attention and limited resources to
solving known problems, especially by developing reference and
testing materials free of matrix effects.

Major Contributors to This Report

Program Evaluation and Methodology Division

John E. Oppenheim, Assistant Director
Phillip R. Herr, Project Manager

Denver Regional Office

Debra J. Carr, Senior Evaluator

Ordering Information

The first copy of each GAO report and testimony is free.
Additional copies are $2 each. Orders should be sent to the
following address, accompanied by a check or money order
made out to the Superintendent of Documents, when
necessary. Orders for 100 or more copies to be mailed to a
single address are discounted 25 percent.

Orders by mail:

U.S. General Accounting Office
P.O. Box 6015
Gaithersburg, MD 20884-6015

or visit:

Room 1100
700 4th St. NW (corner of 4th and G Sts. NW)
U.S. General Accounting Office
Washington, DC

Orders may also be placed by calling (202) 512-6000
or by using fax number (301) 258-4066, or TDD (301) 413-0006.

Each day, GAO issues a list of newly available reports and
testimony. To receive facsimile copies of the daily list or any
list from the past 30 days, please call (301) 258-4097 using a
touchtone phone. A recorded menu will provide information on
how to obtain these lists.

United States
General Accounting Office
Washington, D.C. 20548-0001

Official Business
Penalty for Private Use $300

Address Correction Requested

Printed in the USA
CPSIA information can be obtained
at www.ICGtesting.com
LVHW071501241123
764822LV00012B/550